About the author:

Andy Kind has been a stand-up comedian since 2005. Originally from Newcastle-under-Lyme, he now lives in Manchester.

The Gig Delusion is his second book, following on from
Stand Up And Deliver: a nervous rookie on the comedy circuit

Praise for Stand Up And Deliver

"Totally unputdownable and our book of the year!"
Sorted Magazine

"A funny and very honest book. I laughed out loud. It left me wanting to know more."
David Nobbs (creator of Reginald Perrin)

"Meticulously accurate, entertaining, surprisingly moving. Kind projects an accessible, warm, upbeat demeanour that makes for an easily enjoyable read."
Chortle.co.uk

Andy Kind

THE GIG DELUSION

A NOVEL ABOUT DOING COMEDY

Wilmot
Books

ISBN 978-1-905691-13-5

A CIP catalogue record for this book is available from the British Library

First published in 2013 by Wilmot Books

       Wilmot Books
       http://www.wilmotbooks.co.uk
       info@wilmotbooks.co.uk

Printed and bound in Great Britain by
Lightning Source Inc, Milton Keynes

This book is for Rebecca Elizabeth Hancock

Contents

Prologue

"Can a man still be brave if he's afraid? That is the only time a man can be brave."
George R.R. Martin

For as long as I can remember, I wanted to be a comedian.
I had proved over the last few years that I *really* wanted it. Travelling the length and breadth of the country for a pittance, performing to aggressive, disinterested and non-existent crowds, I had not so much thrived as endured.
But now, finally, I was there. I was earning money - enough money to ensure that the stuttering, disparate evenings in front of a microphone could now rightly be termed 'a living'. It was still, perhaps, premature to entitle it a career, but it was at least a job. My job.
I was a comedian.

And I needed an agent.

This story starts at Manchester Piccadilly station. I don't know if you're aware, but the name Manchester actually derives from two olde Saxon words: 'Manch' meaning 'less pretentious' and 'ester' meaning 'than London' (Actually, Manchester means 'breast-shaped hill', but if you can find any comedy there, you're a better man than me).

I took an early train from Piccadilly, and six episodes of *Family Guy* and a change at Euston later I heard the train manager announce: 'We will shortly be arriving into London Waterloo.' I don't want to start this book by slagging off other professions, but he probably could have just said 'Waterloo' there. I doubt that any man, on hearing he was arriving at 'Waterloo', panicked that he'd entered the melee of the 1815 battle and defenestrated himself.

Getting off the train, I strode along the platform with the other commuters, treating it a bit like a Formula 1 race, trying to overtake as many as possible and mentally commentating like Murray Walker. A mad-looking woman in her seventies approached me in the chicane.

'Excuse me, do you know a Mr. James Purdock from Somerset?'

'I'm sorry, I don't know him,' I confessed, and walked on, pretending it was a pit stop.

Leaving the station, I turned left down the Embankment, checked the map, swore, turned round and went the other way. I was already having a rubbish time.

After twenty minutes of anxiously walking down blind alleys and trying to turn right along roads that had never existed, I eventually found the street that I had asterisked on my map. Slowing my pace to get my breath back, I observed with mild bemusement the hordes of people hurrying to get to work: suited and booted graduates racing to jobs they didn't really want to do so they could work longer hours than their bodies could cope with to impress people they didn't really like so they could get promoted to a higher pay scale...and then work even longer hours and spend too much time away from people they did like so that eventually when they retired they could have two years of luxury before the inevitable death by heart attack (...and breathe).

It was a world now so alien to me. Like lots of people fresh from University, I'd ventured into the City looking to cash in my soul for £40,000 OTE. Fortunately for me, the figurative cheque bounced and I got out almost in one piece. A life of 18p beans and charity shop spending sprees would do me nicely, thank you very much. My lifestyle choice might return to haunt me when I hit sixty without a pension, but I had started spending a lot of time in parks befriending wealthy-looking pensioners, so the contingency plan was in place.

Walking in the opposite direction from the mass of pretty people-shaped shells, I halted finally in front of a sign displaying the words I'd been looking for: Derek House. Pressing the appropriate buzzer, a disembodied voice soon rang out from the grate.

'Hello, Big Fat Comedy Agency, this is Diane. Who is it please and how can we help?'

I had an appointment to see Carlos, the Managing Director, at 9:30.

'I've got an appointment to see Carlos, the Managing Director, at 9.30,' I said, telling the truth.

The buzzer sounded and I went in and took the lift.

The Big Fat Comedy Agency occupied the sixth floor of what, in my native Stoke, we'd call a skyscraper, but what people in London call a building. The lift doors opened onto a spangly office space, with pictures of various comedians and actors adorning the walls. It was evidently a highbrow institution because there was a Tassimo coffee machine on the receptionist's desk and not just a kettle and some polystyrene cups.

'Hello, I'm Diane, how can I help you today?' asked the receptionist, displaying excellent inter-personal skills and a dreadful memory.

'I'm Andy Kind. We spoke about forty-seven seconds ago. I'm here to see Carlos.'

'Right, and what name is it?'

'Andy Kind,' I said, wondering if Diane might actually be a highly evolved goldfish.

'Take a seat, Andy. I'll let Carlos know you're here. Would you like a Tassimo?'

'Lovely, thanks.'

'...Carlos, it's Diane. Yes, I've got Andy Kind here to see you. Ok, thanks, I'll tell him you'll be right over...He'll be right over, Andy.' Diane went back to her laptop and it became clear that she had already forgotten the Tassimo.

About three minutes later (plenty of time in which to drink the Tassimo I was offered and never given), a man ventured out of his office, looking precisely as you would expect a man named Carlos to look.

'Barry?'

'Andy.'

'Come through. Have you been offered a Tassimo?'

'Yes, but I haven't had it yet,' I said, sounding more plaintive than I needed to be in that situation.

'Diane, get this man a Tassimo!'

'Certainly.'

Carlos' office looked precisely like the sort of office you'd expect someone named Carlos to have. The walls were feng shuied with photographs of him shaking hands with celebrities, and some pictures of just Carlos.

'See that one?' He pointed to a photo above his lava lamp, of him with his arm round Mr. Mistoffelees from *Cats*. 'That's Diane, my secretary. She wasn't even in *Cats*.'

'Then why...'

'It's all about image in this business, young man - you have to look the part. Did the make-up myself.'

Offering me a seat, Carlos proceeded to fix me with a long, hard stare. It lasted long enough for Diane to make me a Tassimo – something she singularly failed to do.

'So!' Carlos eventually broke out. 'You'd like us to take you on as a client, would you?'

'Well, ideally, yes. I've been going for a few years now and it's going pretty well, but I really feel that having an agent could help me get to that next stage.'

'What next stage?'

'Er...I suppose just doing bigger gigs.'

'Why us?' Carlos shot back.

'Well, I've heard you're one of the best.' It was a sentence usually reserved for tempting bodyguards out of retirement, but Carlos smiled approvingly.

'Also,' I continued, 'my style is quite similar to some of the acts you already represent.'

Carlos went to stand at the window with his back to me.

'You realise most of our acts are London-based. It's the only place to be for comedy. How would you feel about moving to London?'

'Yeah, that would be fine – I love London,' I replied. Had I been Pinocchio, at this stage my nose would have impaled Carlos through the heart and smashed through the window, spouting glass and guts onto the street below and leaving a legacy of lasting psychological damage on the passing Londoners. (NB. This is not to besmirch Pinocchio himself, who I'm pretty sure used his powers mainly for good and hardly ever for executions).

Carlos turned sharply and jutted a finger in my direction. 'Do you know the worst thing about comedians?!'

In my own personal, non-libellous opinion, the worst thing about comedians is that some of them are Jim Davidson.

'Erm...no?'

'Lack of commitment, of course. Lack.of.commitment. I once got a comedian a slot on Sky News, and he said he couldn't do it because of a family holiday. Had to let him go. You don't have family, do you?'

'Well, no, not at the moment, but...'

'...Just as well. It's a single-man's game, comedy. It demands to be your first love, not some floozy, second-hand hooker on the side.'

I was starting to get the impression that this was Carlos'
signature speech – the one he made to all the young bucks who
ventured into his domain.

'Commitment is what we need,' he continued. 'Co.mmit.ment.
You suck my c*ck, I'll suck yours. Not literally, that would be
disgusting...' he broke off and shot a wide, self-satisfied grin in
my direction.

'I'd be very committed,' I offered, trying not to retch.

'How do I know, though?' Carlos enquired, throwing himself
into his high-backed leather seat. Clearly I'd taken the bait, and
now here came the denouement.

'We don't *need* any more acts, Gary.'

'Andy.'

'But we are always on the lookout for committed acts.
Commitment, above talent, is the one thing that makes a
comedian great.'

I disagreed, and decided to stand my ground.

'I agree.'

An ominous smirk traced its way across Carlos' face. This was
the moment he always looked forward to, clearly.

'A challenge, then. A gauntlet, if you will.' He licked his lips,
savouring the power he fancied himself to wield. 'There are
thirty-nine counties in England. Thirty-nine. You have ten
weeks – ten weeks! – to do a gig in every single one of them.'

I tried hard not to let my face look like that emoticon with the
squiggly line (this one ~).

'Complete this task, and we'll gladly take you on and help you
become great. Fail, for whatever reason, and you're not the man
we're looking for...Goodbye!' Carlos boomed, slapping his hand
hard upon the desk in front of him. He had enjoyed every
moment of that.

Somewhat dazed, I shook Carlos by the hand and made my way
back into the lobby.

'Thanks for the Tassimo,' I said to Diane, ironically.

'You're very welcome. Take care, now.'

The lift doors opened.

Recalibrating myself back on street level, I tried to get my head around the precise nature of Carlos' challenge. Was it a wind-up? Surely, nobody was going to pull off something like this.

And maybe that's the whole point?

Carlos didn't really want me as his act – of course he didn't. He'd set me a challenge that was so unfeasible that he could rest assured I would fail, while at the same time claiming to have given me a chance.

And I would surely fail. No, I didn't have a family yet, and comedy, for long uninterrupted stretches of my life, would rightly have been called 'my first love'. But all that had changed. Comedy had been knocked off top spot by a new apple of my eye. And in ten weeks – the time I had to complete this task – I would marry that apple (who, in non-figurative terms, was a fully-functioning woman).

The thing to do was march back into the Big Fat Comedy Agency, thank Carlos for his patronising offer of patronage, and leave with my dignity intact.

But then something stirred. A foolish, pig-headed defiance – the same defiance that forced me onto the stage on that wintry first night down in Bath several years before, and the same defiance that had compelled me to press on after every bad gig since – dug its heels into my psyche and said, quite simply, 'Let's 'ave it.'

I would go back to Manchester and plan my campaign, determined to wipe the smug grin off Carlos' face. First, though, I would go straight to *Argos* and order a Tassimo machine...

**

A few months previously...

I was taking Betty to Edale: to propose.

I'd wanted to get my proposal right. Everyone hears about those dreadful public proposals, like the poor bloke in the States who disguised himself as the team mascot at a basketball match, staged a scenario whereby his girlfriend found herself on Centre Court, revealed himself and proposed...only to watch her – along with several thousand other people – run off into the night. And thanks to Youtube, he can watch it again whenever he likes, as well as countless other videos, with sympathetic titles like 'Guy proposes on live TV...EPIC FAIL...hahaha, loser, WTF bro?!!!'

So I had planned it carefully. Romantic yet dignified, and free from cliché – and above all, somewhere that, if she said no, no one would see and I could escape into the hills to live as a wildman.
Edale would do perfectly.

I picked Betty up at 10:00am and we headed east out of Manchester along the A6. Betty knew we were going to Edale for the day, but I hadn't told her I was going to propose because I wanted it to be a surprise (Call me a radical bohemian nonconformist if you must).
The weather all that week had been, at best 'dour', at worst 'Will you please stop f***ing raining?!!' The forecast for today was 'grim' (or to translate that for people south of Watford: 'northern'). But as we wound our way through the village of Disley, the sun burst through the morning cloud and carpeted the road ahead with glorious sunlight.
'Wow, look at that,' exclaimed Betty, dramatically. 'It's like God wants us to go to Edale!'
I mouthed a silent prayer skywards, thanking Him for the break

in the weather and demanding that He not give the game away.

There were other practical issues that could go awry. What my prospective wife didn't know was that I'd hired a minstrel. And when I say minstrel, I mean 'travelling' and not 'chocolate' or 'black-and-white'. I wanted my proposal to be chivalrous, rather than 'calorific' or 'grossly racist'.

I had a friend called Hayley who used to be a comedian, but who now travelled the country busking and writing songs. The grand, convoluted idea was that Betty and I would go for a walk around Edale, crossing the start of the Pennine Way (the longest footpath in Britain, so if you're planning on starting a long journey together...are you with me?) In the plan, we would return to the village for lunch, at which time I would text Hayley to notify her. Subsequently, she would accost us by the little Norman church and entertain us with a fable about the local area – the end of which led neatly into the proposal.

But what if Hayley broke down on the way?

What if Betty says no?

I parked the car in Edale village, we donned our walking boots and I packed a small rucksack with the only items I had that might be useful for hill walking: a small length of rope and an apple.

The chill in the air felt quintessentially English, exhibiting the chastising sternness of an Edwardian nanny. And off we went, passing The Old Nag's Head pub where, all being well, we would later eat lunch, and out towards Kinderscout - a windswept upland gritstone plateau, the tallest peak in the district of the same name (Thank you, the Internet).

All was proceeding according to plan. We walked a couple of miles, stopped for a flask of tea, continued. The mental checklist was accruing ticks by the minute, and I was starting to relish the imminent drama. And then, when we reached the point at which I'd planned to about-turn and head back to Edale, I tried to text Hayley.

I stood there, dismayed, looking aghast at my phone as it revealed a problem I hadn't foreseen: I had no signal. Even amid the bracing chill of this January morning, sweat started forming on my brow and trickling down my back. What was I going to do?! I had no way of telling Hayley when we would be back in the village - no way of even knowing that she was there in the first place. I continued to stare at my phone in angry woe (It's the same look I use when people I've long respected tell me they support Tottenham).

I needed to move. Snatching a half-full beaker of hot tea from Betty's hand, burning her mildly in the process, I packed away the flask, threw away the apple core and put the erroneous emergency rope back in the bag. Then, trying to maintain some slight modicum of composure, I squeaky-barked, 'Right, shall we head back then?' and started off down the track. Betty looked confused, bewildered and in pain from the scolding hot liquid I'd splashed on her. She got to her feet and started coming after me, with purpose rather than compliance.
'What are you doing? Why are we heading back? This is my day as well, you know. Why did you pour tea on me?'
I didn't possess the answers she sought, and all I managed was a 'We'll be late for lunch!' slung at her in an over-the-shoulder way as I galumphed off horizonwards.

Then she started crying.
'Andy!! Stop running away. If you're having a rubbish time with me, just have the guts to say so – don't just make excuses!'
Oh no, please stop!
'We've come all this way, and I was enjoying it, but all you seem to care about is yourself. This relationship won't work if it's just you in the centre of it.'

I don't recall my exact thoughts at that moment in my life. If I had to wager, I'd guess at something like 'Oh ******** ****, **** ***** ********** ***** ****.'

What was I supposed to do now?

All I could do was keep on moving back towards the village, trying to skim placatory, half-mumbled sentences in Betty's direction. But how about this: the closer we got to Ground Zero, the longer Betty went without an explanation for my waywardness, and the greater therefore the chance of me getting back to the church and proposing to a girlfriend that I no longer had!

It was a bit like being behind a gritter on a motorway. You know you have to get past it somehow, and that you're going to get gritted no matter what, but there's the choice between going cautiously and getting more grit, or speeding past and getting gritted hard. I suppose you might say that, regarding the gritter situation, however you proceed doesn't threaten to ruin your prospects at life-long happiness. And you'd be right - this is a messy analogy for a messy situation.

I strode onwards, recklessly trying to get back to the village, anxious not to get too far ahead of the woman I loved and upon whom I had inflicted third degree tea burns.

'Andy, I feel sick,' Betty moaned.

Edale village and its church spire were on the horizon, moving closer. I could sense a vicious face full of grit was on the other horizon, approaching at the same speed.

'A lovely pub lunch will cure what ails ya!' I responded, sounding like a medieval tosser.

Finally, finally, we re-entered the village and limped past The Nag's Head, totally dishevelled and out-of-breath. (NB. I have cleverly edited the part where I failed to navigate a stile and fell painfully on my bottom, hurting my pride and my bottom.)

Now I just needed to remain cool.

'Ooh, I could do with a sit down. Could you do with a sit down? I know I could - let's sit down.'

'The pub's not even open yet, you weird man. What is wrong with you?' asked my future former girlfriend. She shook her head ruefully, like she'd been cast in a shampoo advert but the fee wasn't great and her heart wasn't really in it.

'Well,' she said with a tired huff, 'we might as well go and sit on that bench by the church.'

'Yeah, OK, good idea, great!' I said excitedly, as though I'd somewhat unexpectedly been drafted into a shampoo advert after the original actor withdrew, citing irreconcilable differences.

She hadn't broken up with me. Now she was offering to go and sit where I needed her to sit. This was happening.

As we slumped on to the church bench and I tried to throw Betty off any possible scent by talking a lot about scampi, I realised that I couldn't see Hayley. I'd been so concerned with getting back in time that I hadn't thought about what would happen if my minstrel wasn't there. Now I did, though. To make matters worse, the landlord of The Nag's Head unbolted the pub's front door and erected an A-board with the daily specials.

'Right, shall we go and have some lunch then...' Betty smiled.

'Erm...I'm not sure I'm that hungry.'

'What?! You've just spent ten minutes straight talking about scampi. I've never known anyone talk about scampi uninterrupted for that period of time. I didn't even know it was possible.'

'Oh well, you know, you can talk yourself out of these things, can't you...'

I braced myself for grit.

Then I heard a guitar.

'Ooh, what's that?' wondered Betty.

A red-haired woman who used to do comedy came strolling nonchalantly round the side of the church in full minstrel dress, strumming away and saving my scampi (bacon). I have never been more pleased or relieved to see someone with a lute. I could have married Hayley at that moment – which would have been woefully counter-productive, I admit.

Hayley introduced herself as the travelling minstrel, and offered to let us be the first people to hear her new song about Edale. I squeaky-blurted that we would, sounding far more excited than I have ever sounded before or since about listening to a song (I include all songs by Will Smith).

You don't need to know the exact wording of the song, but in essence it was a story about an old man's will, a female sheep used in a trade agreement, and a young Derbyshire lady named Mary Mee. I'd written it myself and emailed it to Hayley, who had valiantly committed it all to memory.
The final line of the song was, 'So, here endeth the story of the *will*, the *ewe*, and *Mary Mee*,' at which point Hayley turned to face us and said, albeit hammily, 'Hang on – that sounds like "will you marry me"...doesn't it, Betty?'
Betty looked at me, suddenly understanding.

I'd spent years travelling the comedy circuit, pinned under the intense scrutiny of thousands of pairs of eyes. I welcomed it; but this solitary, beautiful pair made me feel more exposed, more vulnerable than all the others combined. Several times a week, I performed to audiences in excess of two hundred punters; but this audience of one made me feel like I had nothing to say.

Emit words then, you medieval imbecile...
'...I'm sorry I scalded you with hot tea. And I'm sorry I dragged you back here without warning. And thanks for not laughing at me when I hurt my bottom. And will you marry me?'

I had taken the potential eloquence and poetry of a simple proposal, and kicked the shit out of it. In none of the reveries in which I'd imagined this going down had I ever conceived of prefacing 'Will you marry me?' with 'I hurt my bottom' (I could picture the Youtube title: Man proposes by talking about own botty...EPIC FAIL...hahaha, loser, WTF bro??!!!)

What I had forgotten, of course, was that I was loved. In spite of my ear-splicing stupidity, I was loved.
And she said yes.

(NB. Again, I've cleverly edited the part where I burst into tears and the minstrel just stood there looking uncomfortable.)

Then we went to the pub, and I had a burger.

T-Minus 10 Weeks

"To achieve great things, two things are needed: a plan, and not quite enough time."
Leonard Bernstein

I drive.

There's a thousand comedy clubs in this country. You give me a time and a place, I give you a twenty-minute set. Anything happens in those twenty minutes and I'm yours, no matter what. Anything happens a minute either side of that and you're on your own. I don't bring a mic. I don't host the meat raffle. I drive...and then I do the gig...and then I drive home again.

I had a lot of work to do if I wanted to achieve this hasty goal of gigging in every county in England. While I knew of existing gigs in lots of the places, I wasn't sure what sort of comedy, if any, was on offer in Hampshire or Sussex. Plus, if I'm completely honest, the existence of a county called Rutland made me wonder whether the cartographer had just put it in for a joke and hoped no one would notice.

I was clueless as to what I would do in the event that no available gigs existed in a particular province. Worse, there are over a thousand working comics in the UK today. You can't just ring up a promoter and say, 'I'll be in your neck of the woods next week – can I go on last?' Well, if you're Michael McIntyre you can, but not if you're Andy Kind. This whole endeavour might well end up less a Comedy Roadshow and more a Caravan of Disaster.

Still, as I have always said, 'You can't do Gig 39 before you've done Gig 1' (It's a phrase I imagine seeing attributed to me in a book of famous quotations some day). And so I took the first of my '39 Steps' with hope rather than expectation, by getting in my battered Ford Fiesta named Florence and driving to Worcester.

I coasted down to the South Midlands with the other acts on the bill, all of whom lived in Breast-shaped Hill. On the journey, I divulged my plan to perform in all thirty-nine counties in ten weeks. All three of the comedians thought it was an exciting challenge. Not one of them had heard of Rutland. Some of us needed to spend more time browsing Google Maps (safe search moderate) and less time on Google Images (safe search off).

'It's going to be tough to do, Andy,' said Ray Kane, a Yorkshireman whose hairline was even more conservative than mine. Sitting alongside me in the passenger seat, he'd done some mental number-crunching and worked out that I would need to average four gigs per week (I know the maths for that is fairly straightforward, but we're comedians, not Jonny Ball/Carol Vorderman/someone you know who's really good with numbers).

'It's difficult enough to get four gigs anywhere in a week,' Ray mused, 'let alone in a very specific place. I love your enthusiasm, but I don't think it can be done.'

Dom Woodward nodded his agreement from the back seat. 'Yeah, by all means go for it, but that's a massive ask, that is, Andy lad.'

I burped. I didn't mean it as a response – it was merely pre-journey pork pie starting to repeat.

Both Ray and Dom were right, though, and before I'd even set foot on the first of thirty nine stages, it felt like a losing battle.

But then Victor Smithers, a long-time friend of mine and a man who could always be relied on to offer unhelp, piped up.

'Hang on a minute, brosefs. I think this whole idea needs rethinking.' Victor paused to take a bite of his own pork pie (I'd bought a pack of three and kindly offered him the surplus).

'Anyone can do a gig anywhere at any time if they want to,' Victor continued. 'We could just turn up at a random pub this evening, tell them we're travelling comics and ask to do a gig – we've got a mic and a carload of audacity. Performing isn't the issue – it's the stuff that goes on around it that counts, like having a captive audience and getting paid for it. That's the bit that makes it difficult, but Andy hasn't said that those are fundamental.'

'Thanks, Victor,' I said. 'That's very helpful.'

It *was* helpful, in the same way that offering to carry your mate's rucksack during a freefall would be helpful.

'You know, Vic, that's a very good point.' Dom had been won over, and he was followed sharply by Ray who said something equally annoying about Victor having a good point. I entertained a miniature daydream where I accelerated the car into the central reservation, killing myself but wiping out all witnesses to this conversation.

Victor started holding court.

'Precisely, so I think three things:

1) I probably need to get in touch with your contact at Big Fat Comedy Agency, tell him primarily that you're an average comic and I'd be an infinitely better choice.

2) Insist that he draw up some more specific guidelines to stop you coasting, and...

C) We should stop at the next services so I can have a slash.'

'You changed from numbers to letters there, Vic.'

'I'm aware of that, but I'm so desperate for a piss it stopped being a priority.'

Dom and Ray laughed, and I did another burp.

Worcester, you may or may not know/care, would have been the evacuation point of the British government in the event of a German invasion during World War Two.

As the task ahead threatened to invade into my own life, the gig proved to be a suitable refuge from the oncoming barrage. Held in the Graham Hick Suite of Worcester County Cricket ground, overlooking the river and with the cathedral backlit on the vista, it was packed to the rafters with expectant punters.

I went on first as compere. I was no longer an open spot (a brand-spanking-new act) petrified at the sheer feeling of being on-stage. I was a professional comedian with over seven hundred gigs under his belt. It didn't guarantee success every night of the week, but being on-stage was like a second home these days – a home, albeit, where you sometimes got heckled and abused by hundreds of strangers.

Compering - the guy who hosts the show and introduces the other acts - was the role within comedy that I'd always found most enjoyable and for which I was best known (Actually, I was best known in comedy for being a Christian, but that's not so much a 'role' as a reason for people to avoid car-sharing).

The job of the compere is not so much to be funny as to allow the comedians to be. We call it 'jumping on the grenade' or 'taking one for the team'. Good comperes are very much the unsung heroes of comedy nights, getting and keeping the ball rolling while taking none of the credit. And like any compere worth his salt, here in Worcester I employed the standard warm-up tricks that we 'Masters of Ceremony' use to prep a crowd for a night of comedy - getting them to cheer like pirates and farmyard animals, insulting any nearby council estates, telling any well-preened men that they were gay.

Before I brought Victor on stage to open, I confessed my County Challenge and its resultant predicament.

'So if anyone knows of any feasible venues in any of the other thirty-eight counties, please do let me know,' I said, with my tongue slightly in my cheek.

Two hours later, as we were packing up for the drive back to Boobymound, a tall, wispish man with a face like a handsome shovel strode over to me from where he'd been standing at the bar. I feared he was a disgruntled inhabitant of an abused nearby council estate, and wanted to put me in the ground - something for which his attractive shovel-face would have been perfect, as it happens.

'So, this challenge of yours – you got anything lined up for Devon yet?'

I'd managed to stave off assassination for another day - phew. Also, this sounded promising.

'Frankly mate, no,' I replied, 'and I'm already starting to think it was a dreadful idea.'

'Well, if you do go through with it, give me your number. I run the occasional night down there – I'm here visiting my brother. I'd be happy to hook you up.'

'Oh right, well, thanks, mate – stay in touch,' I said, touching him in the form of a handshake and nearly calling him Spadeface.

On the way back to Manchester, we complimented one another on a good show, in the slightly masturbatory way that comics do when they're sharing a car.

'Yes,' started Victor Smithers, 'I think we were all equally good, but I think I was arguably more equal than the rest of you. And even if I wasn't, I surely deserve extra points for that George Orwell reference.'

We allowed Victor to have his glory, and refused to stop at the services the next time he needed a wee.

The next day, Victor did indeed call Carlos, shortly after which the agent sent me an email with a list of 'Carlos' Commandments'.

Carlos' Commandments had been attached to his email in a Word Document, written in the French Script font to make it seem more archaic. The Commandments were thus:

1. You must perform a gig in each of the 39 English Counties within 10 weeks of today's date.
2. Each performance must be no shorter than 20 minutes in length.
3. You must receive payment in excess of £25 for each performance.
4. There must be an audience of at least 20 people (humans only, no animals)
5. Photographic evidence of the gig and venue, and a phone number for the organiser, must be provided.
6. You must wear clothes for each and every performance.
7. If you exceed the period of 10 weeks, for whatever reason, that counts as a fail.
8. If thou dost succeed, thou shalt have no other agent but me.
9. You must never pass my details on to people like Victor Smithers ever again.
10. See the above 9.

I'd created a large wall-chart in my bedroom, crudely sellotaping eight pieces of A4 together and scrawling on the names of all thirty-nine counties using a fat nib. It looked totally crap, and so I just reversed an old Euro 96 wall chart that I found in the loft.

'Are you sure about all this?' asked Betty (or FutureKind as I'd taken to calling her since we got engaged). I was over at her house and we'd just finished another exciting instalment of our favourite game, whereby we sat at one end of the living room, deliberately gave ourselves pins and needles in both feet...and then had a race to the kitchen. I couldn't wait to get married so we could play it every day.

'Really, are you sure you want to do this? It sounds a bit far-fetched.' If she'd been my wife already, this would have been a wifey look.

'Yes, my lovely, I'm positive. Getting an agent is what I need to take me to the next level of my career. Better gigs means more money, which means more money spent on Wifey. It's a hunter-gatherer thing.'

'My love-language is quality time, not gifts. You should know that by now. I'd rather have my husband around all the time, not turning up once a week with fur coats and those little partially-haired dogs.'

'I promise not to bring you a partially-haired dog, whatever it is that you're on about.'

'Good. It's still not great timing though – we haven't even finished planning the wedding properly.'

'Look, futuristic wife, it'll be fine. My ability to provide for us in married life will be greatly improved once I get this agent, and I'm mature enough to balance gigs with wedding planning.'

'You've just had a pins and needles race across the living room, and called me gay when I won. I'm not sure that you're as mature as you think, my love.'

'...You aren't!' I said, winning.

She kissed me on the cheek and smiled sympathetically.

As I sat there, the feeling slowly returning to my lower body, I was convinced that I could complete this County Challenge, but re-reading the list of necessary destinations brought home just how difficult a task this was going to be. Who did I know in Northumberland? What gigs were there in Wiltshire? Where the fuggering buck was Rutland?!

In my diary I already had gigs booked for thirteen of the counties, but that still left me with a massive shortfall and would mean a huge amount of ringing round and scrounging if I were to climb all 39 Steps. Still, I'd nailed Worcestershire, and the day after that I was able to draw a big black, felt-tippy line through Shropshire.

Now, before I started writing this book, I had fanciful daydreams of dedicating an entire chapter to each of the thirty-nine separate counties. There are, on reflection, two problems with this. Firstly, not every gig I do is eventful. In fact, most gigs I have ever done are what you might call 'uneventful': *I drove to the gig, I did the gig, people laughed somewhat, I drove away from the gig*.

The second problem with having a chapter devoted to every single leg of the tour is that, on a personal level, it would mean more time writing and less time taking a nap. I can't operate under those conditions.

So, sorry to disappoint all you Shropshire fans out there, but I'm going to treat it like people from Shropshire treat Wem – by skirting around it and never breeding with its inhabitants.

It's not that I don't have a gold-plated, Shropshire-coated anecdote in my armoury - far from it, compadre. I once spent a weekend just outside Ludlow on a Duke of Edinburgh Bronze Award expedition, circa 1995. I got chased by a bull, sworn at by ramblers, and set fire to my tent and a close friend. However, none of that is pertinent here, and while the gig in the wonderful town of Shrewsbury for the wonderful Kevin Bland was wonderful, it can, unlike the upcoming Kent venture, be reduced to this simple formula: *I drove to the gig, I did the gig, people laughed somewhat, I drove away from the gig, avoiding Wem.*

And I'm afraid that's all the coverage Shropshire will be getting. As a further line of defence, Salop (Shropshire's former name) is also a French slang word meaning 'slutty', so it would be better all round if we just drew a line under this whole affair.

The above is one of those quirky facts that you pick up when you travel around the country on the comedy circuit for long enough. I have others. For instance, without having to research it, I know that Reading has the world's biggest lion, a stone monument to the 19th Century Afghan wars. I will never need to know this information. I don't know why or how I know it. (There's also an outside chance that these back-to-back morsels of trivia are so dull that, even now, you're considering putting the book back on the shelf and picking up a Danny Wallace. Go ahead, it's no less than I deserve).

The flipside to this doubloon is that the human brain can contain only a finite amount of information, and so, while I might not want to remember the fact about the monumental lion or the salacious border county, the date of my parents' anniversary has been unceremoniously ejected to make way. My brain operates a strict one-in, one-out policy.

That Saturday I took my mindful of pointless tidbits with me down to Berkshire's 'capital' for a gig in the hometown of comedy supremo, Ricky Gervais. The Gervais Effect has obviously paid off down there because the people of Reading had donned their handbags and their gladrags and turned out in force (People who gig in Newcastle-under-Lyme will find that the Kind Effect has been minimal, if that).

I shared the bill that night with Paul Kerensa and Jo Enright. Jo has starred in most British sitcoms over the last ten years, while Paul has written for most of them. I've done neither, and so my name was featured in a slightly smaller font on the promotional posters for the night:

The act of being on-stage and making audiences laugh until they hurt themselves can occasionally serve to convince you that you are in some way important. There's nothing like seeing your name in Size 8 Brady Bunch font to make you realise that is a vicious lie.

However, the major benefit of gigging with TV names is that the punters tend to come to the event, not just in their droves, but also with their breath pre-bated. There are only two ways that an audience member can approach a gig: ready to laugh or determined not to. Having people like Jo on the bill means that the former scenario, while not guaranteed, is much more likely. After all, who isn't impressed by a Size 22 font?

It was a tonking gig, and the fact that someone approached the comedians at the end, asked for Jo and Paul's autograph and then asked me where the toilet was didn't really matter that much. It's no big deal. I'm not even sure why I'm talking about it to be honest with you. I'd almost forgotten it had happened until you mentioned it just now.

So it was three good gigs from three. Don't worry, that sequence will never befall us again.

**

When talking about being a comedian, the microscope tends to focus on the joys of being on-stage – the public face of stand-up. But often, there's as much fun to be had off stage as there is on it.

On the drive back north from Berkshire, I experienced one of my top petrol-station-based episodes of all time. That may seem like nothing special, but, without wanting to sound too much like Alan Partridge, in 2002 I shook Todd Carty's hand on Knutsford forecourt. Top quality handshakeage.

I pulled into Cherwell Valley services to fill up the tank, restock on pork pies and have a large tinkle. It seemed, on the surface at least, to be a perfectly standard pump-based episode. I played the system a little bit, removing the nozzle from its housing before unscrewing the petrol cap, thus eradicating a potentially frustrating waiting period as the cashier turned on the pump. It's one of many time-saving devices I use on my travels, such as stocking a meaningful packed-lunch, or weeing into a modified Capri-Sun during traffic jams.

I queued up inside the kiosk. Behind the counter was a man who looked – and probably smelled – like he had watched every episode of *Robot Wars* at least twice. His hair was so lank and greasy that it made me think deeply about peak oil. His bedroom wall was almost certainly bedecked with posters of 'thinking man's totty' – Phillipa Forrester, that Rachel woman from *Countdown*, Professor Brian Cox.

Superficially, the fact that he was clad in brown leather jacket and checked shirt might suggest he was at the more fashionable end of the geek spectrum. But in the way that all socially peripheral humanoids do, he had managed nevertheless to look profoundly unfashionable, his clothes offering a keen hint of 1970s Slavic detective.

But then, without warning or prior consultation, this pongy cashier in Serbian raiment blew open my expectations.

The woman at the front of the queue handed over a pack of mints and said 'Pump 4, please.'

'That comes to £14.75,' responded the man, who was probably called Norman or Colin. Nolin.

The woman ferreted around in her bag for change, but was then distracted by a bombshell from Nolin.

'Battle of Vaslui.'

'Sorry?' asked the woman, still, appallingly, failing to find the right money.

'Battle of Vaslui, 1475,' Nolin reiterated, visibly exasperated that the woman had no idea what he was talking about. 'Stephen III of Moldavia defeats the Ottoman Empire, led at that time by Mehmed II, the conqueror of Constantinople.'

'Oh right, that's good knowledge,' the ferreting woman replied, politely.

'It's my job,' stated Nolin, nasally and incorrectly.

The woman shuffled off, replaced by a bloke in his early twenties, who hadn't tanked up but had stopped solely to invest in a boxed set of chicken sandwiches (a scenario he could have bypassed had he given any modicum of thought to a meaningful packed-lunch before travelling).

'18.15,' said Nolin, his face teeming with confidence. 'Battle of Waterloo.'

'Nice one,' said the bloke, not bothered.

None of the other queue-dwellers seemed at all fussed by Nolin's performance. But I was loving it. Nolin had taken the boundaries of working in a petrol station, stretched them to breaking point, then told them to piss off.

The next two people in the queue were duly given, in turn, instant trivia about the year correlating to the price of their purchase. Nolin was like a human, reliable version of Wikipedia (one where I'm not reported as finishing second in a World Ferrero Rocher Eating contest to Timmy Mallett).

Nolin was blowing my mind, to the point where my life insurance premium would have gone through the roof (if I understood what life insurance was, or was capable of thinking ahead in any way).

I was next into the fray. If anyone has ever been more excited while queuing to pay for petroleum, I've not met them. The way ahead clear, I approached the desk with a mingled sense of trepidation and giddiness. Nolin's thick, uncleansed hair shimmered like an oil spill. It was a barnet, ironically, dense enough to have smuggled refugees out of war-torn Yugoslavia, if only the U.N. had known.

Nolin looked me in the eye. I returned the greeting. We both knew what was coming.

'Pump 7,' I said weightily.

'That comes to...oh..30.45.'

Nolin's face fell: my heart sank.

'I'm sorry,' Nolin confessed. 'It doesn't work with the future.'

We looked at each other, crestfallen. There was no queue building behind me and so we dwelt on the moment together. Had there not been a massive wooden counter between us, I think I would have embraced Nolin, even though it now became clear that he did smell absolutely and without question like a man who has watched every episode of *Robot Wars* at least three times – possibly back-to-back.

Simultaneously, as Nolin's musk threatened to destroy my olfactory capabilities, a brainwave hit me.

'What do you think might happen in 3045, though?' I asked, like a moronic child.

'Oh...well, now then...let me see, let me see...' Nolin's mind started fizzing. I could sense his mind plunging into the unknown abyss of historical events yet to come. Then it came:

'...The combined armies of New Germany and Womanland fight off a superior force of sexy Russian Cylons in the Battle of Dingbat Mound.'

I gasped. Nolin stared at me triumphantly.

OK, his prediction got weirder as the sentence went on and there were strong hints of sexual perversion that needed sustained counselling, but I thought it was a cracking attempt.

'I only regret I won't be alive to see it,' I said with a sense of reverence.

Nolin nodded. We bade each other farewell, and I left.

It's vignettes like that which make long comedic return legs worthwhile. I would meet Nolin again, by which time I hoped he would smell slightly less like a Balkan sweatshop.

It's people like Nolin who make life worth living. But for every wondrous person in the world, there has to be, according to physics, an opposing turd of equal force. I made contact with the latter of those that evening.

I was a week into my ten-week agent-coveting challenge, and three of the '39 Steps' had been climbed. I emailed Carlos the report from 'T-Minus 10' and he rang to tell me I was already behind schedule, and to remind me again that com.mit.ment was what he was looking for.

Personally, I was trying to be more optimistic. Thirty-nine gigs over ten weeks can't be broken down into 3.9 gigs per week. A gig is either a full gig or it's nothing. To my way of thinking, I had simply rounded down one week to three gigs, and would now simply have to round up the next nine to four gigs. On paper, that might sound reasonable, but also on paper – or rather, in my diary – I didn't have four gigs per week.

Most of the necessary counties were, as yet, untapped. Plus, I had a wedding to plan for and a fiancée to keep happy: all big challenges for a man who only merits a Size 8 font.

**

Grandad sat on the orange velour sofa with his legs squashed beneath him.

'So, you see, son, you just sit here for a while until you start to lose the feeling, and then you get up as quickly as you can and run to the kitchen. Right, you have a go.'

'OK, Grandad. But what if I fall and hurt myself.'

'Oh don't worry about that – I'll catch you if needs be.'

Gran came in from hanging out the washing and reprimanded her husband.

'Oh, don't teach him that game – it's ridiculous.'

'Nonsense – it's a bit of fun, isn't it, son?'

'Do you want a race, Gran? I'll give you a head start.'

'I certainly do not. Don't let your Grandad teach you bad habits.'

'Bad habits? He's eight years old. Did you want me to teach him how to weld?'

'I just think you might set him a more mature example. Now come and have some lunch, both of you.'

I got up, couldn't feel my legs and started toppling. Grandad caught me, we both started laughing, and he helped me hobble into lunch.

T-Minus 9 Weeks

"And all for love, and nothing for reward."
Edmund Spenser

I had an evening off, and Betty and I were watching a film. It was her turn to choose, so it was a film with Hugh Jackman, but not one of the good ones where he is a Wolverine – and thus I hated it.

'Will your ushers be staying over on the night before the wedding, or will they all turn up on the day?'
Betty had a ring-binder open in front of her. Strewn around her was an array of lists, graphs and floor-plans. She was either in wedding mode or was plotting the invasion and outright destruction of a small European country.
'Will your ushers be staying over on the night before the wedding, or will they all turn up on the day?' She didn't ask this again – I'm merely using it as a device to help you remember what she said in the first place. You're welcome.
I was thinking about Carlos' Commandments, and didn't answer.
'Will your ushers be staying over on the night before the wedding, or will they all turn up on the day?!!!' Now she did say it again, and with a lot more menace than before. If she were planning on taking down Andorra or somewhere like that, then that's the tone she would use.
'I would have thought they'll all just pile down on the day,' I replied. 'It'll be fine.'
Betty frowned.
'But then they won't be able to help with the set-up on the Friday night, will they? What's the point of them being ushers if they can't help out a bit? You can't expect my bridesmaids to do

it all!'

What Betty had done, you may have noticed, was to use the old 'question that isn't really a question' technique. Her question: 'Will your ushers be staying over...' wasn't really a question at all. It was a statement – a statement which would have been better phrased thus: 'Your ushers *will* be staying over on the night before the wedding, and none of them is allowed just to turn up on the day.'

'I'll let them all know, sir!' I barked.

'Sorry, honey,' Betty softened, 'I'm not trying to give you orders. But if you're going to try and do this gig challenge, then we need to have the wedding stuff sorted well in advance, don't we?'

Even when she was reprimanding me, she had a way of making a rebuke seem like encouragement. I couldn't wait to marry her. From the moment she'd said 'Yes', I'd been constructing our future in my mind. Granted, in my mind it was a future that involved flying cars, wise-cracking house-robots and basically being *The Jetsons*, but the desire to be with Betty for the rest of my life was genuine, real and good source material for a film trilogy.

I wanted to provide for my family, and she was it. I had no idea how to secure gigs in most of the outstanding counties, but getting an agent would ensure better gigs for more money and help me build my reputation as a comic. That was the reason I wanted an agent in the first place. For my family. For Betty. (And to help towards a downpayment on that house-robot, whom I would name Dean).

The next day, I found myself sitting in a closet with two male strippers and a seedy man with a massive erection. I should probably bolt some backstory on to that sentence.

**

My friend Tony Vino ran a series of comedy nights under the banner of Just Funny People (JFP). I'd phoned Tony while waiting for the sales assistant to bring my Tassimo from the *Argos* warehouse in London.

'Kindy, Kindy, Kindy!' he exclaimed, employing the only greeting he had ever used in five years of friendship (The solitary occasion he rang up and said simply 'Hi, Andy', I was convinced it was Robert Patrick from *Terminator 2* and spent two days hiding out in a local motel).

Tony was due to be my Best Man at the wedding and I trusted him with my life. I also trusted him to place me into excruciating social situations on a bi-monthly basis (he once booked me as the warm-up act for what turned out to be an evening of Gregorian chanting) and so, when he offered me a gig in Chatham Docks that coming Monday, my hopes weren't orbital. Nevertheless, I had to take gigs where I could get them. I'd be able to tick Kent off the makeshift Euro 96 wall-chart, and there was the offer of a road trip with my bestie. And it would probably be fine. #noitwouldnt #yes_im_using_hashtags

Having been vomited out of the M25, we (me, Tony and Victor Smithers) dutifully followed the instructions of my sat nav, Debbie, until we were 1.0 miles from our destination. In the same way that you can tell a man by his shoes, you can usually tell what sort of gig you're going to have by the local environs.

'Don't worry,' said Tony, 'I'm sure this post-apocalyptic scene with wheel-less cars and numerous things on fire will soon give way to rolling countryside. You'll see, by the time we get to 0.3 miles, we'll see bunting and street parties.'

When we got to 0.3 miles from the venue, Tony had started writing a will, while the sound of *Radio 2* was being drowned out by the chopper blades of a police helicopter directly overhead.

I've seen the film *Black Hawk Down* and, not being a member of Delta Force or the US Rangers, had always felt fairly confident I'd never have to re-enact it. This view was now up for appraisal as we parked and watched ninety or so men with hatred in their eyes and tattoos in their eyes stop what they were doing – which was standing menacingly in a pub car park – and turn towards us, as surely as a snake turns towards a mouse that has been dropped into its glass cage. The smell of waste gas started to fill the car from three separate vents.

'Is there any chance either of you has superhuman powers that you've been keeping needlessly quiet?' enquired Victor.

The three of us exited the car and I locked it, hoping that I might suddenly look at the key fob and see, next to the buttons for 'lock' and 'unlock', a previously unseen button with a picture of the Batmobile on it. I didn't.

We walked into the venue with as much dignity and boldness as it's possible to have when you're emitting so much gas, it feels like you're deflating.

'Keep a tight perimeter,' Victor mumbled through unmoving lips.

'Their vision is based on movement,' Tony added. I smiled inadvertently, accidentally making eye-contact with one of the tattooligans as I did so.

'What the f*** are you smiling at?'

'Sorry,' I mumbled, and stepped over a dead dog.

'Are you the f****** comedians?' boomed a voice as we lurked around the reception area.

'Yes, pal,' asserted Victor, who seemed to be the most confident of the trio – in that he was able to respond using words rather than mere 'fnnnh' sounds.

'You better be f****** funny. They're not laughers, by and large, this bunch.'

Before any of us had a chance to ask one of the many questions that had suddenly sprung to mind, this guy continued, 'Your dressing room is down the corridor, third on the left – you're sharing with the strippers.'

'You're a wonderful man,' gushed Victor, already breaking into a full sprint. Tony and I looked aghast at each other, then trudged off after Smithers. So a few moments later, Tony (married), me (soon to be married) and Victor (sporting a substantial hard-on) sat in our empty dressing room, experiencing emotions ranging from horror to 'Maybe there is a God', hoping – two of us for a quick death, the other for an experience that he had previously been happy to pay for.

Then the strippers arrived.

'Oh, hi boys, didn't realise we were sharing.'

The name they gave to their stage act was Ebony and Ivory – presumably because their real names of Scott and Errol weren't quite sexy enough.

'You're not sexy women,' Victor said flatly.

'Well spotted,' said Scott (Ivory).

'Thank God,' puffed Tony.

'That's a relief,' I added.

'Well, what I am going to do with this now?' Victor said, looking down.

Once the bittersweet anticipation of sharing a closed space with semi-naked ladies had been dispatched like the seamless trousers that Scott was wearing, a more seditious prospect raised its glittery head. Comedy is not at its most successful when trailing in the wake of strippers (of either sex). When an audience is sexually charged, the last thing it wants is whimsy. It really is lose-lose.

A male comedian following a male stripper is going to get shouts of 'off, off, off' – as in 'Take your clothes...' When this doesn't happen, he is going to get shouts of 'off, off, off' - as in 'Get the f***...'

Taking this gig now seemed like the worst idea since Geoff

Capes thought, 'Hmm, I wonder how strong my teeth are...ooh look, a massive lorry and a length of rope!'

'Let's go,' I mouthed at Tony.

Tony nodded ruefully.

'Are you the only strippers on?' Victor was pumping Ebony and Ivory.

''Fraid so, but don't worry, we'll warm them up for you.'

'Vic, shall we go?' Tony suggested to Smithers as the strippers went behind a screen to put on glitter.

Victor harrumphed. 'To be fair lads, this looks like a 100% guaranteed nightmare, but it's £150 that I can't do without.'

'Do you want to make £150 this way, though?' asked Tony.

'Well, now that I'm here, yes. Plus the fact, Tony, that you've got a kid on the way, Kindy is about to get married and...sorry, I can't think of a third – I'm being distracted by this huge boner.'

Victor took a breath and continued. 'Look, we all need the money – and Andy, what other gigs are you going to get in Kent? We have to stay.'

We all looked at one another. Victor was right – we did need to stay.

Eight minutes later we were back in Florence the Fiesta, handbrake-turning our way out of Dodge, laughing uncontrollably and call-diverting the promoter's attempts to bring us back.

In fairness, after Victor's pep-talk, we had decided to stick it out, take the money and run. I would try, I had resolved, in my conversations with Betty and the rest of the known world, to omit any reference to sharing a bill with male strippers. Then, however, through the stage door, we heard the unified chimes of sixty women chanting expectantly:

'Get your wangs out, get your wangs out, get your wangs out for the girls...'

Something about pulling out just in time.

**

As Jerry Seinfeld says, good gigs help you explore, bad gigs help you edit, and gigs in Kentish coastal towns help you gently along the road to ketamine addiction.

There are times, as a comedian, when you can convince yourself that your current set is water-tight. A run of good gigs releases so many endorphins that it acts like morphine, bequeathing you the wholly irrational idea that you will never struggle on stage again. But then you turn up at venues like the one in Chatham, and you realise that you are about as equipped for the job as my fiancée would be for invading a small European country.

The journey down to Kent, within the context of Carlos' challenge, counted for absolutely diddly nothing. I hadn't performed, and there was no way of contriving it so it seemed like I had. I also sensed that the previous night's event wouldn't be the last to fall into the category of 'misadventure'. I needed to be ready if it did happen again.

And so, the day after Kent, I sat down at my desk and started the most frustratingly glorious of all artistic endeavours: writing new material.

Every stand-up comedian needs to write his own material. This is an opinion, but it's an opinion I respect and I think we all should. Stand-up comedians are primarily comedy writers who perform. If you want to go on stage and use other people's material, become an actor.

The process of writing varies from gagsmith to gagsmith, of course. Some people get up early, drink an entire family-size cafetière, and then sit at a computer screen frantically tapping away while the caffeine overtakes them and nymphs and centaurs skip gaily around. Other comics wait for something incongruous to happen to them, blitz in a few jokes and then road-test it on stage. Neither method is particularly easy and both require work. Very occasionally a joke will appear fully-sculpted. Too often, you have to chip away at an indefinable block of an idea for ages.

Inspiration is a coy mistress. In fact, maybe she's more like a cat. Most of the time you can't find her, no matter where you look, but then every so often she'll appear and come and sit on your lap (I'm sorry if that sounds a bit weird or surreal: I've just finished an entire family-sized cafetière and there's a unicorn looking at me through the window. It's very distracting).

So, the morning after the Kent before, having got up at 7.30am, showered, breakfasted and watched five hours of terrestrial television, I eventually sat down at my desk with a big sheet of blank paper...and waited for inspiration to come. A further three hours later and the same sheet of paper was covered with a Top Ten list of 'Weird Totty', a detailed sketch of a wee-spurting willy, and the first scene of a play about lumberjacks. So it was going well. Stupid inspiration cat.

At 6:00pm, despondent about my stand-up, but confident that my new dramatic work 'We Have Axes' would be a West End smash, I downed tools (pen) and drove to Staffordshire, the so-called 'creative county' – which has certainly struggled with its own mental block over the years.

The Staffordshire leg of this bow-legged tour was, by several country miles, the easiest to arrange - not least because the gig there was only several country miles away from where I was invented.

In the county town of Stafford, there happened to be a real dingledodie of a gig. Down a back street, off the main square, lies a quaint drinking tavern named 'Joxer Brady's'. On the first Monday of every month, since the ice melted enough for Britain to isolate itself from mainland Europe, Juice Comedy had run an open-mic night for acts new and old to come and sharpen their tools (not pens). It was run by a duo of foppish gents called Neil Reading and Rob Halden, both of whom I would pay to be friends with, though haven't as yet had to.

Neil is one of the nicest men in comedy, whose infectious enthusiasm had kept Juice Comedy Club ticking along for nearly a decade. Rob Halden, a spectacular misanthrope of a man with a beard of Blessedian proportions, might be one of the best comedians you'll never see, given his almost spiteful refusal to perform anywhere outside Stafford. That said, it was his curmudgeonly rants that had kept the steady trickle of local punters flowing back month after month.

The morning after Carlos had gleefully emailed me the rules for the County Challenge, I made the first of a series of clamouring phone calls to friendly promoters in my address book, desperate to scrounge and scrape whatever gigs I could. Neil had picked up and said he'd be delighted to slot me in for the coming week's gig, so long as I mentioned in print the fact that he was 'one of the nicest men in comedy, whose infectious enthusiasm has kept Juice ticking along for nearly a decade.' I said that wouldn't be a problem and we booked it in.

The rules of Carlos' game (as you know, gentle reader) state that 'Each performance must be no shorter than 20 minutes in length'. Only the headliner at Juice does that length of set, and so Rob Halden graciously yet disgruntledly agreed to step down from that berth. I asked him how I could make it up to him, and he told me I could start by referring to him as 'one of the best comedians you'll never see, whose curmudgeonly rants had kept the steady trickle of local punters flowing back month after month.' I said that wouldn't be a problem and we shook hands and nearly kissed.

The population of Stafford is 65,290. Of that number, 65,273 had made alternative plans for the evening. Juice Comedy was attended, as it always was, by seventeen punters. To the untrained eye, or anyone with eyes, this might not seem like that many. But in a culture that sees so many new comedy gigs starting and, shortly afterwards, falling by the wayside, there is something really lovely about a gig that never gets any better nor any worse. Ever. A gig that, like a brute fact or Brian Blessed's beard, is just there.

The modest turn-out certainly didn't faze the group of young comics on the bill that night, nor did the voice amplification system that came courtesy of a miniature karaoke-style speaker resting precariously on a wonky bar stool. James Acaster and Paul Savage both stood out from the crowd, although you probably won't know who I'm talking about – unless you've found this book in the back of an attic in 2030, in which case you'll be like, 'Woah, no way, dude, those guys are awesome, wow!'...I imagine. I also imagine you'll own a wise-cracking house-robot, but I shall say no more about that henceforth.

The real upside to a gig with a small but loyal following (or 'Speaker-on-a-chair gigs' as I like to call them) is that the atmosphere in the room is much less pressured and brittle than at bigger gigs, and you can therefore be a lot more playful in your approach. It's like having a swimming pool lifeguard who not only allows diving, bombing and heavy petting, but cheers you on and films it. Large audiences, by contrast, appear like an amorphous sea in front of you, and you just have to swim with the tide. At "biggigs", you never really engage with persons - just people.

At the end, I thanked the audience individually and joked that, unlike a bespoke comedy club where you rarely make eye-contact with punters, here at Joxer Brady's we'd probably all stay in touch. If you remember, Commandment 4 of Carlos' Commandments stated that there must be an audience of at least twenty people, while 5 was: photographic evidence of the gig and venue, and a phone number for the organiser, must be provided. With the previous gigs, I'd simply taken a photo of myself in front of the bustling audience, then emailed the promoter's details to The Big Fat Comedy Agency. The issue at Juice, to which I've alluded, was that seventeen punters falls short of the minimum. To make up the deficit, Neil and Rob ventured out into the night air and rounded up four random passers-by with, in Neil's case, the promise of a free half-pint and, in Rob's case, the threat of unrequited heavy petting. Subsequently, the photographic evidence for the gig came out like the cast photo for a defunct soap opera - a soap in which four of the actors looked surprised and a little frightened to be there.

**

Later that week I had long-booked-in gigs in Westmorland and Suffolk, both of which passed without incident and, most crucially, without spontaneous erections or strangers press-ganged into collusion. I would have met my quota of four gigs for the week, if only the gig in Kent had been a gig and not the plot of a low-budget porno.
I've learned a lot in nearly a decade of doing comedy. The main lesson I've learned is this: gigs that aren't gigs shouldn't be gigs.

As I reached the end of Week T-Minus 9, no manner of rounding gigs up or down could help me. I was officially one gig behind schedule, which meant that at least one of the ensuing eight weeks would need to be filled with five gigs - and taking for granted that they all happened and didn't end in Mogadishu-esque extraction.

I sent Carlos the report from the week. He sent back the following perfunctory email:

```
Re: Kent — LoL.

Already behind schedule, I see. No shame
in quitting whilst you're only marginally
behind. Have   you   given   thought   to
becoming a stripper? Plenty of work about
from what I hear.
I've attached a photo of a cow looking
upset. I saw it and thought of you.

I say again - LoL.

Carlos.
```

He had a point (though not about me resembling a sad cow). I'd climbed only six of the 39 Steps and already I was looking like a wheezing, panting Homer Simpson of a character. This was actually the reverse of LoL (...which is still LoL – curses!) I needed help – some sort of figurative Sherpa to drag me up to the summit. Or an actual Sherpa, but I think they might be mythical and I don't have time to check. Colon, dash, open brackets.

The figurative Sherpa came in the form of an actual childhood hero of mine. As I sat at my desk, staring flatly at the ominously unblemished underside of the Euro 96 wall-planner, I got a call from Tony Vino.

'Kindy, Kindy, Kindy!' he exclaimed, reassuring me that it was him and not a cyborg dressed as a policeman pretending to be him (I no longer had the budget for errant nights in motels, after all).

Vino went on to tell me that he'd been due to go on the radio the next day, but had to pull out because of...well, who cares?

'Kindy, you can go on and plug your challenge. Andy Crane says that's fine.'

'OK, that sounds...sorry? Andy Crane?'

'Yo.'

'As in *the* Andy Crane? Poor man's Philip Schofield, but rich man's Toby Anstis?'
'Yep, the same. Have a good'un!'
Semi-colon, dash, lower-case p.

Andy Crane, as you must surely know, was the second most famous of Children's TV presenters from the golden age of kids TV: the 1980s. And don't try to disagree. After Pip Schofield left CBBC and Gordon the Gopher was put down, Andy Crane and his mate Edd the Duck made that broom-cupboard their own.
And now I would get the chance, not only to meet a childhood hero, but also to plug my comedic needs to several thousand people. As I would have said at age eight, this was mint.
'This is mint!' I said at age twenty-eight, and then, reneging on all decency, I did the Bartman.

**

'I'm so excited!' I told Betty on the phone at 6:00am.
'Why are you ringing me? I'm asleep.'
'Because I'm going to meet Andy Crane today!'
She put the phone down.
When she finally answered her phone three hours later, I had lost none of my excitement.
'I'm awfully excited, Betty! I nearly cried during my Weetabix.'
'You keep telling me. Look, it's a good opportunity, but don't get overawed and say something stupid. You won't ask him the question, will you?'
'What question?'
'You know what question - the question that every former child now in their late twenties asks him. The one he's probably sick to the back teeth of hearing.'
'Of course not. I'm not that stupid.'
'You are that stupid, my love, that's why I'm reminding you. Whatever you do, don't ask how Edd the Duck is. Or where he

is, or what he's up to.'
'Look Betts, it'll be fine. I'll call you after.'

Betty was right: I was that stupid. Plus, I didn't have a good track record with children's TV presenters. The year before, I'd done a gig in Lymm and Matthew Corbett of Sooty fame was in the audience. During the break, he stood next to me at the urinals and I asked if Sooty had a willy, then caught him with some splashback. *#fact*
But this would be fine. I had another conversation ace up my sleeve for meeting The Crane - I'd heard that Andy Crane once entered an Andy Crane lookalike competition, and came fourth. I'd open with that.

Having left the children's screen with a gold-coated legacy well in place, Andy Crane was now to be found hosting a current affairs show every Sunday on *BBC Radio Manchester*, broadcast from the Lowry Theatre in Salford Quays. The show's producer Emma met me as I arrived, and I placed an order for two cups of coffee. I've kind of made that my thing when doing media stuff. After all, who are you going to re-book, the dullards who have a single cup of coffee or the maverick who obliterates the status quo by asking for two cups of coffee? I think you know.

As I was part way through coffee 1.0, Andy Crane approached me with all the self-assurance of a man who knows he's nailed the last three decades.
'You must be Andy,' said Andy Crane.
'So must you,' replied Andy Kind.
Andy Crane laughed. I made Andy Crane laugh. This was going amazingly well.
'How's Edd the Duck?'
Nope, I'd ruined it. I'd essentially gunged myself.
Andy Crane grimaced and looked mildly put out. *Come on, Kindy, win back the audience.*

'Andy Crane, did you once come fourth in an Andy Crane lookalike competition?'

'No.'

'...Good, I didn't think you had.'

Andy Crane went off to talk to the other guests, who hadn't got overstimulated by getting a laugh, asked about an erstwhile puppet and then tried to fall back on erroneous trivia.

The radio show itself was rompingly good fun. There was a lot of talk about politics and I don't know very much about politics (I thought Mugabe was one of the Pokémon). I only really know about comedy and 1980s children's TV, but I'd prematurely shot my load in that department and so I sat silently, feeling totally hammered on excessive amounts of coffee and nodding feigned comprehension. During one of the music interludes, I decided I needed to apologise to Andy Crane.

'I'm sorry about the Edd the Duck comment, Andy Crane. I just got excited to meet you. You're a bit of a hero.'

'Oh, don't worry,' soothed Andy Crane. 'You get used to it. And 'I don't know' is the answer to the question. He's probably in a different broom-cupboard, being used as a mop.'

'How the mighty fall,' I quipped. Andy Crane laughed again. I'd made Andy Crane laugh again. I'd done it - I'd won back the audience. *Well done, Kindy!*

'Are you still in touch with the other guys - like Andi Peters?' I was on firm footing now. The other guests sat silently, loads shot, waiting for the conversation to veer back towards politics.

'I bump into them from time to time, yeah.'

'And Otis?'

'Otis? The aardvark?'

'...Yes.'

'Well, he was a puppet, too.'

'Wasn't there a man in there, though?'

'No, just a hand - like Sooty or Orville.'

'Seriously?'

'Yes.'

'Are you lying?'

'No!'

'Oh...'

Come on, Kindy. Bring it back again.

'...I tinkled over Matthew Corbett once.'

Nope, gunged myself again.

The major good to come out of the show was the plug for my challenge, which got a number of encouraging texts from listeners and an abusive text from a man calling himself S. Vmithers. Andy Crane suggested I come back in a couple of months and tell them how it had gone, which was incredibly gracious given my conversational autism. It did mean, though, that the County Challenge was now out there, broadcast to a large slice of the nation. I had lost my chance to squirm out of it, and one of two eventualities lay before me: heroic success or regional ignominy. I would either succeed, and be carried shoulder-high around the cobbled streets of the North West by celebrity chef Simon Rimmer, or else I would fail, and be driven deep into the sewers to live as a self-elected rat oligarch. To my mind, those were the only two alternatives.

It had to be the former. I didn't want to come back on the Andy Crane Show in a few weeks and say, 'No, sorry, I bottled it...oh, and by the way, have you got Postman Pat's mobile number?'

Tony Vino was philosophical about it. 'At least you didn't slash on him, Kindy.'

True. I was making progress.

**

Grandad was seated on the yellow velour settee, sipping tea from a translucent cup and saucer, while I was sitting cross-legged on the floor facing the TV. I was meticulously sorting out the 'gots' and the 'needs' from the twenty-four packs of Panini stickers that Grandad had bought me earlier that day, then painstakingly unpeeling the wrapper and smoothing the stickers onto the album. For a nine-year-old boy, twenty-four packs of stickers was like a bank heist. Unable to process the sheer joy on receiving them, I had pulled down my trousers and pants and flapped my willy like a lunatic.

I had since calmed down.

The continuity presenter on the television was bantering playfully with a small puppet sporting a garish green mohican. Grandad chuckled with mild incredulity.

'Nothing like that in my day,' he said, taking another slurp.

'Grandad? Why is Gran at work and you aren't?'

'Because I'm a bit older than your Gran and I've retired.'

'What does that mean?'

'Well, it just means that I'm too old to go to work, I suppose.'

'What did you do before you got too old?'

'Well, I was in the army for a bit, and then after the war I worked in a bank.'

'Was it fun?'

'Not really, no. I wanted to be on the stage really - 'treading the boards', we used to say - but my parents said it wasn't a proper living so I never did it. What would you like to be when you grow up?'

'Hmmm...either a fireman, or Lion-o. I haven't decided yet.'

'Well, no need to decide just yet - oh look, your Gran's home. Don't do that thing with your willy again, please.'

T-Minus 8 Weeks

"It's when you know you're licked before you begin, but you begin anyway and see it through no matter what."
Harper Lee

The coverage on the Andy Crane Show reaped instant dividends (I'd love to follow that sentence up with 'And now I'm hosting a rebooted *Knightmare*', but sadly not). The day after the radio show, a woman from Whitley Bay rang up to book some comedians for an event that same week. I agreed with gusto and was far too busy dissecting Northumberland on my wall-chart to upholster myself with any information besides postcode and time of arrival (In truth, I was also distracted by grief that the *Knightmare* dream was finally over...unless I bank-rolled it myself...?)

'But we've got our Marriage Preparation course tomorrow night,' Betty said, wiping the smiley emoticon off my face.
'I know, but I need to take these gigs, my lovely. I'll make the one next week, and I'll come round and vacuum your stairs or buy you a partially-haired dog.'
I went in for a consolatory smooch. Betty pulled off a sidestep that would have made it into a Six Nations highlights package and looked away, her lips pouting slightly, as they always did when she was sad.
'Betts? Why have you Brianodriscolled me? I've said sorry...'
'You haven't actually,' she corrected.

I looked at her interrogatively and, for an instant, thought I noticed a gentle crease of fear around her eyes...but it quickly ironed out to a familiar look of patience. She gave a deep breath and said:

'Look…of course you can go and do your gig, but I don't like the idea of you changing our existing plans. It's not fair on me and it's not a good precedent to set. When you say 'Yes' to something, that should mean 'Yes'.'

'Well I've said 'Yes' to this gig now….'

Then I had an idea that only a comedian would have had.

'I could double up!'

'What?'

'I could double up – I could open at Marriage Prep and then go and headline the Whitley Bay gig.'

'Open? Headline? Honey, not everything can be equated to comedy. Marriage Prep isn't a gig. It's nine people in a living room – that's not a gig. No, go and do the actual gig, but promise me we will absolutely go next week.'

'You're a fine woman! And yes, I promise. Would you like to watch a Hugh Jackman film, but one of the good ones where he's a Wolverine?'

'No, I would not – and besides, we've got another problem.'

Betty opened the mammoth Filofax marked 'Wedding' and looked vexed. Moldova put its citizens on high alert.

'What problem?'

'We've invited too many people to the reception. I've just had the quote back from the caterer and it's a bit more than we can afford.'

This was indeed a botheration. In the days following my critically acclaimed marriage proposition, I got so excited about the prospect of not dying alone that I failed to filter the initial wave of invites. On the very night of the proposal, for instance, at a gig in Rawhide in Liverpool, I invited the seventy members of the audience – a handful of whom had got in touch since to ask what the details were.

'What are we going to do?' I asked (observing the castration of my self-financing *Knightmare* revival by the goblin of this new financial quandary).

'Well, we're going to have to hope that some people drop out,' Betty puzzled. 'And if that doesn't work, we – by which I mean you – are going to have to let people down.'

'Me? Why will I have to do it? I'm busy.'

'I'm not the one who invited Twitter.'

I'd neglected to include that, gentle reader, but 'twas true – I had invited everyone on Twitter. Only Dean Gaffney had got back to me so far.

How do you tenderly inform someone that you no longer want them to share in your special day? That reads like the set-up to a joke, but it will have to hang there without the elusive punchline. This was potentially going to lose me a lot of friends – something which, ironically, if I'd done it pre-emptively *before* sending out the invites, would have eased my current predicament.

I've never been good at breaking bad news. I once looked after a friend's dog while he was touring Australia. Within a fortnight of his departure, the dog massively died and I was left to find a way of passing on the terrible tidings. I put it off for two weeks, deleted my Skype account and tried to replace Milo with an exact replica (something which only works in 80s sitcoms). In the end, I tried to usher my friend gently towards the bad news by starting the conversation with '…You know how some dogs are allergic to fire?'

So the idea of culling people from the wedding list didn't fill me with gaiety.

Later that evening, the phone went and I heard my friend G-reg crying on the other end.

'She's left me, Andy. After four years, she's ended it!'

'Aw, mate!'

G-reg (real name: Greg), a merchant banker who'd quit his job to go and work with endangered animals, had been in a relationship with a woman for four years – a horrendous woman who nobody liked apart from G-reg.

'I couldn't believe it,' he continued in splutter. 'She said now that I'd lost my job she was embarrassed to be with me...said she didn't want to be with someone that smelled like a panda.'

'Aw, mate!' I said. There are only really two things you *can* say to a mate who cries down the phone. One is 'Aw, mate' and the other is 'Chin up'. I thought I'd save the 'chin up' bit until the end of the conversation – you know, finish with something inspiring.

G-reg snotted his way through all the reasons why this was the worst thing that had ever happened to him. I said 'Aw, mate' a lot and then concluded, as planned, with a 'Chin up.'

'Thanks, mate – that's really helpful,' he finished.

'Greg and Amanda have broken up,' I divulged to Betty.

'Oh dear, that's awful!' she said.

'Amanda won't be coming to the wedding.'

Betty and I high-fived.

**

I had five gigs in the diary for T-Minus 8. One of them was in Burton, which falls agonizingly to the left of the Staffs/Derbyshire border and therefore wouldn't count. If none of the others was cancelled, I would remain one gig behind schedule, but I would at least meet the weekly target for the first time. It would be solid evidence to put before Carlos – and myself – that I was still in the mix.

I parked outside Tony's house at 4pm and tooted the horn. It worked as well as tooting a car horn can ever work suburbanly, by scaring a jogger and causing an old Bangladeshi man to think

I was saying hello. Moments later, having being forced to exit the car to explain to the old Bangladeshi man that we hadn't met, two shadowy figures came bounding down the garden path towards Florence the knackered Fiesta.

Despite not once offering to drive, I would, it transpired, be chauffeuring two fully grown men (both with better cars than me) to a gig in Whitley Bay that I knew almost nothing about, except for the fact that it was in Whitley Bay and I knew nothing about it...except that it was Whitley Bay-based.

'Why am I driving?' I asked, peeved.

'Claire's got our car,' Tony replied.

'I have a frozen hand,' Victor stated.

'A what?!'

'A frozen hand, Andrew.' Victor held up his hand to show me. He was holding it in the shape of a claw.

'Victor, that's not even a thing.'

'Certainly, it is. It's a frozen hand. I couldn't possibly drive with a frozen hand – it would be dangerous. Now come on, or we'll be late.'

So off we went, Victor's hand miraculously back to its normal disposition by the time we turned out of Tony's road. I knew a frozen hand wasn't a thing. As we turned down an adjacent road, we passed a car that looked almost identical, both in terms of make and registration number, to the car Tony claimed his wife was using for the evening.

Morons. That was two wedding invites that could be revoked for a kick-off.

Pumping ourselves out of Manchester before the arterial-road-clogging of rush hour, we spent the flabby excess of time before the gig visiting *The Angel of the North*. Aside from going to football matches with no shirt on, there can surely be nothing more emblematic of the North East. It's poignant and haunting and beautiful, and it certainly encapsulates Gateshead as a place: even the angels wear body armour.

We arrived into Whitley Bay and my sat nav, Debbie, informed us that we had reached our destination.

We were faced on either side by a row of houses. Houses just like any other. Not special, magical houses that morphed at the flick of a switch into bespoke comedy clubs. Houses.

'What the hell do you think you're playing at, Debbie?!' I berated my sat nav. That's the issue with personifying pieces of electronic equipment – in all the excitement, you forget they lack a fully-evolved inner ear.

'Well, what are we going to do now? We're already late!'

I couldn't afford to miss the gig. Nowhere on Carlos' Commandments did it say that simply driving *into* the county qualified as successful completion.

'Has anyone got a number for the promoter?' Tony asked.

'No, just the postcode,' I replied.

'*The* postcode?' Victor barked. 'Surely you mean '*a*' postcode. If we had '*the*' postcode, we wouldn't be having this conversation, Kindy?'

I was feeling stressed out, not quite 'to the max' but definitely in the same electoral district as 'the max'.

At that moment, a front door swung open and a lady with hair like former Arsenal star Ray Parlour came walking towards us.

'Are you, by any chance, the comedians?'

'Er...yes.'

'Well come in, come in, yes? We were starting to get worried.'

We, the comedians, were only now starting to get worried. We followed the lady into what looked from the outside like a fairly ordinary terraced house. However, as we stepped over the threshold, we found ourselves standing inside a totally ordinary terraced house.

Sitting around in the front room was a group of about nine people. In fact, it was exactly nine people – estimates only really work at proper comedy nights that aren't in people's houses.

'Are you OK to use the toilet as your Green Room?' Without waiting for our answer, the woman opened a door and revealed a box-room with a loo and a bookshelf.

Minutes later, Tony, Victor and I found ourselves crammed into a tiny lavatory, like clowns in a mini but displaying more pathos. Both Victor and Tony were whispering insults to me.
'What the hell is this, Kindy?! You said it was a gig!
'I thought it was! The woman rang me up out of the blue and said she wanted some comedians. I thought it would be an office party or something.'
'And at what point did you ask, "Is it an office party?"'
'Well, I didn't. Look, we're here now – we might as well try and enjoy it.'

The 'gig', if we can call it that (which we can't and mustn't) turned out to be a 53rd birthday party for a woman named Violet – the former Gunners' midfielder. Not content with going to a nail bar or a *Harvester*, Violet had decided she wanted something a little bit different for her birthday. And so, possessing no working knowledge of the etiquette or machinations of the comedy circuit, she had emailed after hearing me on Andy Crane's show, and then invited a circle of close female friends round for an evening of laughter and tapas.
You may remember Betty chiding me for equating nine people in a living room at Marriage Prep to a gig. She'd laugh when I told her about this. #wouldshebollocks

While our Green Room was the downstairs bog, our 'stage', if we can call it that (which we can't and mustn't) was the intervening door between the living room and the kitchen.
'It's a full house for you!' one of the ladies effused as she dropped a tiger prawn into her face. And she was right - it *was* a full house. It was full of furniture.
I was once again down to compere, if by compering we mean 'standing in someone's lounge, chatting to women on pouffes like an amenable burglar' (Nobody has ever meant that). Victor

was down to open and Tony to headline.

So, as any good compere does, I 'jumped on the grenade', trying to banter away while Violet and her friends heckled me between mouthfuls of chorizo. The heckling wasn't nasty – more a series of incessant questions about stuff I was saying.

What you must never do in situations where you think, 'This can't get any weirder' is to suddenly start thinking, 'This can't get any weirder'. Just as I was coming to terms with the fact that this was all real and I wasn't Dr Sam Beckett trying to put right what once went wrong, the doorbell went and Violet asked me to answer it.

'Would you mind, love? Saves me getting up.'

With my punchline cut off at the punchl... stage, and the last three minutes of build-up ruined, I went to open the door.

'Is Julie here?' The lady at the door asked as I opened it.

'I have absolutely no idea,' I replied, and with just cause.

'Who is it, dear?' shouted Violet.

'I don't know,' I replied - again, with just cause. 'Who are you?' I asked the woman at the door.

'Linz,' she replied.

'It's Linz!' I trumpeted through to Violet.

'Is that you, Linz?' shouted Violet.

'Yes!' yelled Linz.

'Come in, dear, come in – this is Andy, he's one of the comedians.'

'Oh, hello, Andy – nice to meet you.'

'Hi, Linz.'

'Sorry, dear – do carry on,' Violet insisted, waving me back to the ring. By this time, though, the only thing in the ring was my monogrammed towel and bloodied gum-shield, and so I waited for Linz to get settled and help herself to a mozzarella-filled jalapeño, and decided to let someone else have a bout. I introduced Victor, slapping him sympathetically on the back and handing him a live grenade as I did so.

The ladies cheered wildly - apart from Linz, who was gulping down water and flapping at her chilli-stuffed mouth.

Victor had already picked up on the boxing metaphor, and paraded into the living room wearing a ladies' dressing gown he'd found on the back of the toilet door.

I replaced Victor in the Green Room, reaching the conclusion that, if I was Dr. Sam Beckett, this was the worst episode of *Quantum Leap* of all time and the writers needed immediate dismissal.

'Kindy, don't close the door!' Vino cried out. Too late.

'Ah mate, it stinks in here!!' I gasped.

'Smithers just did a poo!'

'What? A poo?! With you in here?!'

'Yeah, it was grotesque. He made me stand in the corner and turn my back. It was like *The Blair Witch Project,* but instead of murdering me he did a poo. I tried to open a window, but I can't find the key. It won't even flush.'

I tentatively peered over the rim of the toilet, and there I saw it, staring back at me like a scuba diver coming up for air.

'I've flushed six times and it won't budge,' continued the battle-weary Tony. 'It's just sat there.' It was indeed sat there, as though taking part in some sort of #occupytoilet protest.

'Well, we're stuck here now.'

Tony and I stayed in there for the whole of Victor's set, hoping he wouldn't overrun and taking it in turns to retch.

I was only seven rungs up on my 39-Step ladder. Three things seemed obvious as we took the A1 back to Mancunia:

1) I would need some of these gigs to be easier.

2) Victor desperately needed to change his diet.

C) Next time I had a call from a middle-aged woman, I should just suggest a trip to Alton Towers and hang up.

And no, you're absolutely right, Betty didn't laugh at all. She told me to drive round to her house so she could tell me off in person. I claimed I had a frozen hand and couldn't.

**

My next gig ceremoniously ticked Hertfordshire off the list, and was a gig for which I would have gleefully cancelled Marriage Prep or, indeed, been closeted with an unflushed poo.

Tim Vine had got in touch via text. He was due to film his new DVD, *Punslinger*, and asked if I wanted to support him on a couple of the warm-up gigs. The answer involved the rhetorical use of bears, woodland, faeces and a question mark. Opportunities like this don't come along all that often.

I first met Tim at a gig for Paul Kerensa in Guildford circa 2006. He popped along to do some speculative 'new stuff' – which had everyone in hysterics. Some people just got it, man. We didn't get chance to speak much in Guildford because Tony Vino had pretty much farted into Tim's face. It wasn't officially in his face, perhaps – not as though Tony purposely climbed to a height and then swung down at the opportune moment, guffing as he went. But it was disgusting nevertheless and Tim left shortly afterwards, ruining the evening for me and threatening to scupper Tony's entire career because he'd farted pretty much directly in Tim's face. Tim was a big name in the world of comedy, and the thing not to do when you meet a big name – and to be fair, Tony has since learned this – is to fart pretty much straight on to their face.
I decided, therefore, not to take Tony with me to St. Albans - after all, I wanted to be able to chat to Tim without having someone break wind directly at his face.

St. Alban was the first British saint. He was beheaded in the 3rd Century for being a Christian. Still, he never had to meet the offspring of Victor's gastrointestinal tract, so swings and roundabouts.

Tim was already setting up at the theatre when I stalked in, looking around furtively for pagans with hatchets. Most comics just tend to bring themselves – and a guitar if they want to cheat and can't be bothered to write proper jokes.* Tim Vine, on the other hand, brings props, costumes, livestock - anything he can throw into the show, really. He doesn't, however, bring livestock – I put that in because I needed a rule of three. #comedywriting101

Without the gaseous Tony Vino on hand, I was able to chat extensively with Tim about life, comedy and livestock, and for someone so successful I found Tim to be a down-to-earth, engaging man who thrived on making people laugh. Lots of comedians, when you meet them in person, are shockingly divergent from their on-stage persona. The Vinester is just as reassuringly Peter-Panish in real life as he is during a show.

Each member of the audience had been personally invited by the promoter. After all, it was meant to be a low-key pre-season training gig, not a cup final, and so to publicise it too widely would have been counter-productive.

Doing 'warm-up' for something, whether it's a big touring comic or a TV show, is both easier and harder than a normal gig. Easier, because the pressure isn't on you. The audience has come for something specific and so you're just a cheery bonus. Harder, pretty much for the same reason. A comedian requires, above all things, a captive audience. If an audience isn't there for you then you might very well make them laugh, but they won't

---

* This is, of course, me being ironic. Frankly, I'd kill to be as good as Phil Nicol or Nick Helm...in fact, I might kill one of them and take their songs. Bear with me...

really care whether you do or not. You're simply there as the advance guard: the drummer boy at the head of the column, the thinly sliced samples on the delicatessen counter. Unlike other comedy nights, it's not about you, and to try to make it about you is not doing the job.

Not that it ever really could have been about me. That would be like watching a race between a horse and a croissant and expecting the pastry to edge it. Even in his pre-season, lacking-in-match-fitness guise, Tim was still better than most comics at their best.

Comedians don't really laugh at other comics. A couple of years on the circuit is long enough to immunise you against most things comedic, and we are usually too concerned with our own performance, or playing on *Angry Birds*, that the novelty wears off. But every now and then you get the chance to watch, up close, performers who transform something that can feel like just a job into the art form it rightly is.

It's a ridiculous myth, even amongst comedians, that a truly great comic can play to any room. Wrong. That's not the point of comedy. Comedians are supposed to be specialists, not odd-job men. Salvador Dali didn't paint *The Persistence of Time* and then think to himself, 'Hang on, this won't appeal to the armed forces – I'll just draw on a massive pair of tits.'

In comedy, you specialise - you find what it is that you do really well and then you keep doing it. Tim Vine is a brilliant comedian. I don't mean that he can perform to any demographic, any age-range, any room. What I mean is that, when he gets on stage to do the job he's been doing for the last two decades, he almost invariably rips it. And he is all the better for specialising in the sort of comedy he does so well.

It was a great night, the joy of which was diminished only slightly by a punter approaching us at the end, asking Tim for his autograph, and then asking if I knew where the toilet was. There's no business like it.

**

The following day, having been conscripted to gig for some Royal Marines, I yomped down to Weymouth with the amazing Malawian comedian, Daliso Chaponda.

Betty rang me on the way to ask what sort of flower arrangement I preferred for the church interior. I mock-berated her for fretting over such a trifling matter and proceeded to tell her, at length, about the Tim Vine gig. I couldn't see her eyes, so I don't know whether those gentle creases of fear had been re-instated. I suspect they had.

'Can we at least talk about the flowers for a bit when you get back tomorrow?'

'I won't be back 'til the day after, my lovely Futuramabride - it makes more sense to head straight up the M6 to Carlisle and stay with mates there...hello?...I've lost you...no, she's gone - flipping reception.'

Weymouth is rumoured to be the place where the Black Death entered Britain in the 1340s, brought back from France by some dudes fighting in the Hundred Years War. They'd obviously misheard the request to 'bring back some duty-free' for 'bring back a horrific killer epidemic'. Easily done, I suppose. I shared this bit of Black Death trivia with Daliso who riposted playfully with, 'Oh sure, blame the blacks.'

The Marines gig went off with regimental precision. Suffice it to say there were no deaths (black or white).

I finished the week by tabbing up to Cumbria - a county rich with history and culture, and yet known to most Englanders as 'up near Scotland'.

I'd certainly clocked up the miles during T-Minus 8, but as I've told you: I drive. I don't drive, however, when Florence the shabby Fiesta explodes on the way home. Basking in the regal power that crowns a run of lovely gigs, comedy obviously needed to remind me that I am her vassal and not the other way round.

Now, Florence the shabby Fiesta broke down a lot, so it was no biggie in and of itself, but after four nights of gigging on the bounce I just wanted to go home, chat to Betty, eat half a Battenberg and watch *Thundercats*.

I pulled over on to the hard shoulder and speed-dialled the AA. I'd been with the AA for years and, given the regularity with which the Gigmobile broke down, was on first-name terms with some of their operatives. I'd even invited one of them – Oscar – to the wedding and was hoping he might turn up so I could break the bad news about overcrowding in person, having first asked him to put down the wheel jack.

I fished out my membership card and informed the phone operative that the engine was being naughty.

'OK, sir, and have you pulled over onto the hard shoulder and left the vehicle?'

'No, I've decided just to plough on - I'm in the fast lane, powering through. Just thought I'd call to touch base.'

'OK, sir, there's no need to be rude.'

I wasn't meaning to be rude. The adrenaline of a good gig means that you carry on performing for about two hours after you come off stage. Comics are the decapitated chickens of The Arts.

I told her what had happened, and within twenty minutes a shiny yellow van turned up. It wasn't Oscar, but I asked if they could roadside relay a message about the reception. Then I was forced to sit through two verses of *You've Got a Friend* in gorgeous falsetto, after which Florence the patched-up Fiesta limped me home to pink-and-yellow cake and pink-and-yellow cartoon cats.

Some people find the AA a bit cocky when it refers to itself as 'the fourth emergency service'*, but I quite like their confidence. Better to have that as a slogan than, 'Go on, give us a chance!'

Comedy-wise, it had been a positive week. I'd performed with a comedy hero and I had met that vital four-gig target. I was still behind schedule, but I was hanging in. I proudly conveyed my weekly email report to Carlos, and he sent back a picture of a plane exploding.

I would look back in a few weeks and wonder why I had let the gentle creases of fear around Betty's eyes become tears. But then my focus wasn't really on my future wife. The reason we keep comedy as a mistress, after all, is that, for all her flighty flooziness, she knows how to keep us happy.

**

'So, what did you think of her?' I asked my grandparents. By 'her' I was referring to Anna, the girl I just taken round to meet the family. The first girl, in fact, that I'd ever taken round.

The yellow velour settee, still taking pride of place in the sitting room, was starting to look dated, along with the floral curtains that cowered by the windows.

Grandad was sitting at one end of the sofa, chewing belligerently on his unlit pipe and eating Battenberg. The Doctor had told him to cut down, and so Gran was rationing him to one pipe a day, much to the frustration of my Grandad.

'What a lovely young girl!' Gran replied. 'Very pretty, I thought, didn't you?' She looked askance at her husband. Grandad took his pipe in his right hand, removed it briefly from his mouth, and said: 'Too flighty'.

---

* I've heard the Coastguard can't stand them.

'Grandad? That's not very nice.'

'You didn't ask me to be nice, son — you asked me what I thought. I think you'll find she's far too flighty - the sort of girl who doesn't feel like the day is complete until she's fallen in love at least twice.'

'Oh, don't be such an old codger,' Gran chided him. *'He's just grumpy because he can't smoke'.*

'True enough! Bloody rationing — I had enough of that in the war. Nevertheless, what I say is what I mean. I don't mean to hurt your feelings, my boy, but I've never told you a lie and I won't start now. A nice enough girl she may be, but no — too flighty! You'll see...'

T-Minus 7 Weeks

"Fiction is obliged to stick to possibilities. Truth isn't..."
Mark Twain

For FutureKind and PresentKind, it was house-hunting time.

Betty and I were living separately with randomers, but we both agreed that, once we got married, we'd like to move in together. For me, that move couldn't hasten its onset fast enough (and not just because I was excited about playing the pins and needles foot game on a daily basis). My current flatmate, Pob, was a prehensile being who had alighted too soon on the trainline of human evolution - a hominid for whom the title 'homo sapiens' would mean an upgrade to first-class. Jobless, he told people he worked in Equal Opportunities. This meant that he would have sex with absolutely anybody at absolutely any time – but always, always, in the room adjacent to mine. Or in the garden.

The previous day I'd found Pob and his most recent conquest in the kitchen, eating cornflakes and ham and slumped post-coitally (At this juncture, you must feel free to insert your own 'homo erectus' gag. #comedywriting101).
'Andy,' Pob gurned, seedily, 'let me introduce you – this is Sian.'
'My name's Claire,' said Sian.
'You didn't let me finish the sentence,' protested Pob, '...Andy, this *isn't* Sian.'
Claire and I both walked out. It would be great to live with someone slightly higher up the food-chain.

The search for our dream home was far from easy. Being a comedian can be a tough job, but any mirth-peddler can guarantee instant gut-wrenching laughs the moment he rings up an insurer (Sometimes, if I've had a run of bad gigs, I'll go into a bank and apply for a loan – and then throw in some new material while they're on-side). Merge in the fact that Betty worked part-time for a charity, and our house-hunt had been confined to areas of Manchester where mortgage rates were low and car incinerations high.

We traipsed reluctantly from house to house in the wake of an unfeasibly optimistic estate agent, feigning interest, recoiling at miscellaneous smells, being prepared at all times to kick any stray dogs in the face, and basically having a terrible time.

A quirk about Manchester that I noticed as we paraded around property after property is that most houses in the city have four wheelie bins. Four! I'm sorry, but that just seems excessive in an Occam's Razor type of way. I raised this gripe with Futurekind, who shrugged it off with some nonsense about it making recycling easier. This was quite clearly both balderdash and piffle – *more* wheelie bins makes recycling *more* difficult, surely? (Again, Occam's Razor).

My own opinion – an opinion I respect and I think we all should – Is that there is a more vindictive reason for having four wheelie bins. Urban Manchester is a veritable Whacky Warehouse for the city's foxes. Unable to cull them effectively, I suspect the council is trying instead to decelerate their carnage. Subsequently, I think all the houses in Manchester have four wheelie bins so that, when the foxes turn up in the night looking for food waste, they have to play *Deal or No Deal*. This is almost certainly true.

We aborted our house-hunt as evening approached. The houses we liked we couldn't afford, while the houses we could afford filled our nostrils with subtle hints of oblivion. We drove sullenly back to Betty's house, having decided that the most profitable course of action would be to cobble together a massive shoe, install a few windows and start our wedded bliss there. Alternatively, I could snaffle a comedy agent and start getting better-paid gigs, but the shoe thing was out in front for now.

But then, as we were anticipating some consolatory tea and bourbons, Betty noticed a 'For Sale' sign en route that hadn't been there that morning. The idea of looking at any more houses made me want to slit my throat with Occam's Razor, but Betty insisted.

As it transpired, the Turkish man who lived there had put the house up for sale only that afternoon, and we were the first people to view.

We left a few minutes later and, as we halted on the pavement, whispered in conspiratorial unison: 'That's our house'.

'In the middle of our street,' I added, but Betty had never been into ska music and didn't get it.

We were about to embrace in mutual triumph when I noticed a missed call and pending voicemail. I Brianodriscolled Betty's hug attempt and rang through to that slightly odd answer phone woman who might be a robot.

'Andy, hi, it's Jon from GSOH Comedy here – you called me a couple of weeks ago looking for a gig. Listen, mate, I've got a corporate tomorrow that I need an act for. The bloke I booked in has bailed and they need someone last minute - it's yours if you want it. Give me a call back.'

This was exactly the sort of thing I needed to happen if I was going to smash this County Challenge. Betty was still waiting for a hug, but I couldn't let this gig slip through my clutches and go to another act, so I made the call.

There was a slight doubt at the back of my mind as I sat through the ringtones, however. Corporate gigs tend to pay pretty well, and to be short of an act at this late stage didn't seem normative. My spidey-sense, though not in any way repeatable through scientific experiment, was tingling.

'They've halved the fee,' confessed Jon. 'They've got budget issues, but the other lad said it wasn't on and pulled out. You'd really do me a favour if you could do it, mate. I've got other gigs around the country, and I'd try to get you in for some of those, too.'

I agreed. For a corporate, the fee was a thigh-spanking travesty, and the gall of the organisers to try to halve it and still expect the comic to do it was nothing short of fraudulent. Analogously, if you went into a burger joint, paid for a burger, and they then brought you a seeded bap and a gherkin, you wouldn't shrug and make the best of it – and anyone who went in after you would have to be a total idiot.

But I wanted an agent. I didn't want to have to keep touting my arse around the country without representation.

The role of the total idiot in the following scene is played by Andy Kind.

'Good news, honey - I've got a gig tomorrow night.'

Betty smiled without smiling. 'Right, so you'll go after Marriage Prep, will you?'

'Well...no, it's in Luton, so I'll have to give it a miss...'

'Oh, I see.'

'Good, I'm glad you se...'

'...So you don't want to prepare for marriage, then?'

I looked over at the wheelie bins, wondering if any of them were big enough to hide a whole man.

'Of course I do, but it's only one session.'

'No, it's two sessions – you bottled it last week as well to go to a gig.'

Bottled it?

'But it's my job! Do you want us to buy this house, or does the big shoe idea seem like a winner?'

'No, fine. Why don't you book a gig on our wedding day, too? That's only one day, after all.'

Some passers-by were starting to look over at our emergent domestic. I lowered my voice to a strained rasp.

'Look, I've said sorry...'

'No, you haven't!'

'Well, sorry, but you know I'm already behind with this challenge. I need to take every gig. He sent me a picture of an exploding plane, for flip sake! Please don't try to stop me from doing this.'

'I don't want to live here,' she announced at the top of her voice, and flounced off down the road.

'The car's the other way, Betts.'

'I'll walk. You go and do a gig or something.'

Aw-kward. (Director's notes: To be said in a high-pitched American accent).

I didn't see that missing two consecutive episodes of Marriage Prep meant that I didn't want to prepare for marriage. Betty knew that this was a temporary thing – a thing that would benefit her in the long run. Didn't she want me to be successful?

I didn't cancel the gig. I didn't want to live in a shoe. Nobody does.

**

When you spend the better part of a decade travelling the country, you tend to sketch yourself a very diverse social circle. There must have been more, but I can recollect only one occasion where I've stayed in a hotel after a gig (It was after a try-out gig for The Stand in Edinburgh. Jim Smallman and Damion Larkin snuck out during the night and gave all my clothes to tramps). As a rule, I either drive straight home, occasionally stealing an hour's nap in a service station car-park (clutching a rounders' bat to ward off potential rapists) or else I veer to the nearest of my 'ports in a storm' – usually people I've met at previous gigs, who were kind enough to talk to me and not ask where the toilet was.

Subsequently, after scratching Bedfordshire off on the Euro 96 wall-chart, I got in touch with my friend Chris T from Milton Keynes. (NB. His name really is Chris T – this is not an attempt at Bunyanesque allegory). It would be a perfect staging ground for my assault on Luton.

Chris consented to hospitality and asked whether, as a bonus, I'd like to go and watch MK Dons v Bournemouth before heading on. #bears #faeces #woods

Of course I would. Not the most glamorous fixture, but working Saturdays means you hardly ever get to go to football, and the prospect of sitting in the corporate section elicited a funny cooing noise from my lips – like a camp mallard, I would tentatively suggest.

Chris T called back a few minutes later with a bizarre dispatch. Apparently, he'd rung up the Hospitality desk at Stadium MK and the following conversation had unravelled:

Chris: Can I pay for another mate to come too, please?

Random woman: What's his name?

Chris: Andy Kind

RW: The comedian?!

Chris: Er...yes.

RW: No way, I'm a big fan – I've just read his book.

Chris: No, you haven't.

RW: I have. I think he's great. If he's coming, it's all free.

Chris: Is this a wind-up?

Now, you'll have to bear with me on this. I'm not boasting. I should be very clear that this sort of occurrence is a total anomaly in my life. I don't get recognised on my own street, let alone in Milton Keynes. But by some skewed arrangement of cosmic molecules, this lady had indeed read my book and so my drinks, food, memorabilia and match ticket were all on the house. Wow, and indeed, zers.

I have no idea who won the game, so don't bother asking.

I left MK feeling as close to a celeb as I've ever felt or am likely to feel, and my drive to Luton was administered with a self-satisfaction that someone piloting a 2001 Fiesta has no right to exhibit. I also made a mental note to send a copy of *Stand Up and Deliver* to every league club in the top four divisions (I'm yet to hear back from Arsene. Or any of the other ninety. There probably was a problem at the post office or something).

Arriving in Luton was the perfect antidote to the sensation that life was going pretty well. The corporate venue was an extravagant glass-fronted new-build, which in Luton was like the Koh-i-Noor Diamond set into the anus of a donkey corpse.

Comedians despise corporate gigs. They are the modern-day equivalents of being a medieval jester in the stocks. Almost any gig on the comedy circuit proper is what you would call 'rippable' - that is to say, there is a navigable path towards getting the optimum response from an audience. Not so with corporates. You cannot 'rip' a corporate gig. Essentially, you are getting well paid to stand there and be pelted with rancid disinterest.

Charity fundraising balls, awards dinners, Round Table society bashes: the people present at these (largely) black-tie events aren't there to listen to comedy. No, they are there to get totally gazeeboed on free booze. Even the mercurial three-course meal can be a bit of a distraction from the main event: getting totally hammered in the smallest possible time frame. In this sort of environment, a comic is about as welcome as a Jedi Knight at an Imperial Stormtrooper's stag-do, and the most fun you can have is to see how many ladies' shoes you can find lying around after midnight – the owners by that point so paralytic, high-heels become a satanic conceit to be exorcised unflinchingly, and with such gusto that Emmeline Pankhurst would surely weep with pride.

At 7:30pm, as I parked up by the main entrance to the architectural leviathan, a man in a tuxedo was vomiting into a hydrangea as though it had gone out of fashion and then made an instant if somewhat surprising comeback.

'Goodee!' I said with ironic cattiness, sounding like a very upset homosexual.

I introduced myself as the evening's jester and discovered that, in spite of the many lavish rooms in the complex, none of them had been allocated 'green' for my benefit. Instead, a place had been reserved for me with the revellers at one of the huge banqueting tables.

'It'll help you gauge the flavour of the evening,' the ballgowned organiser affirmed.

The flavour was unambiguously that of a dirty pint.

I took my seat and tried to rattle through my set list in silence… but then the bloke sitting next to me wanted to know if I could pass him some more wine and what was I doing?

'I'm just planning my set – I'm the comedian.'

'Oh awesome – didn't realise there was a comedian. Are you like Jim Davidson?'

'…(edited for legal reasons)…'

'Bit harsh, mate.'

Before long, the rest of the table cottoned on to the fact that I was the 'entertainment' and proceeded to pillory me with a series of innovative questions about comedy that I'd never been asked before apart from during every conversation I'd ever had with anyone.

Here we have a prime example of why comedians tend not to be as fun to talk to in real life as they appear on stage. It's not that we don't want people to talk to us – or rather, let us talk to them – about comedy. It's more that we get easily fatigued by the ticker-tape parade of banal questions that get marched out in every social situation. Conversations like that rarely progress to questions about Daniel Kitson's glorious deconstruction of an art form, or the prophetic social commentary of Mark Thomas. If someone I met socially were to ask me a question like that, I might pen them straight into my will.

But no, usually a conversation between a troubadour and randomer goes something like this:

'I'm a comedian.'

'Oh, really? Tell us a joke!'

'No, it's my night off.'

'Are you funny, though?'

'Sometimes.'

'Where do you get your material?'

'From the magic of thought.'

'I tell you who I like: Roy Chubby Br...'

Removes nearest light-fitting and swings it viciously

Some comedians I know won't actually confess publicly to doing the job. So, next time you ask someone their profession and they look shifty and say, 'I do a lot of driving', ask them to tell you a joke and then move away from any nearby light-fittings.

I was due to take the gallows' steps at 8:30pm for thirty minutes of stockaded ignominy. That sounded bearable, actually. Most of them wouldn't be too hammered by then, and so I might leave the stage badly wounded rather than totally cadaverous. But then, having been at the venue for two hours (sipping on water and being force-fed my table's favourite anti-Polish jokes), I was told they were moving the auction forward and I'd be on straight after that. Oh, and someone wanted to give a heart-rending talk about the charity, too, so it would be closer to

10:15pm by the time they got me on.

That was game over. There was no way I was going to survive this ordeal. The crowd would be off their faces, there would be stilettos everywhere, and my warm-up act was now to be an emotional testimony about palliative care. Goodee!

I made a couple of phone calls – to Betty and the Samaritans.

'You don't know, it might be all right,' said the Samaritans.

'Hahahahahaaha. Haha. Ha,' said Betty. I hung up on both of them.

By this stage, the drink alchemists at my table had started mixing orange juice with bottles of astronomically expensive Brunello to make Sangria. They were, quite frankly, blind alleys off the main road of procreation.

I informed the organiser that the gig was going to be excremental in its outcome, to which she replied that she was sure they would be receptive. It was about as feeble a response as claiming that having 'naked ladies' on your web history was a lame attempt at a Googlewhack.

'We'll put you on during desserts – 'cos they'll be listening while they're eating, won't they?'

'No'.

She showed me back to my seat.

And so, Andy Kind, the hero of Milton Keynes, the corporate golden boy of League 1, went on stage at about 10.20pm. He left the stage at 10.40pm, having tried to speak over one hundred and fifty divergent conversations.

At 10.29pm, the organiser, who had revised her opinion of audience receptiveness, came to the side of the stage and tried to wave me off. But you and I know what Commandment 4 states. Anything less than twenty minutes didn't count.

'Just come off!' she mouthed.

'No!'

'Come off, now!'

'No, you can't make me!'

It's difficult to say that it went badly. People have to listen for that to be the case. But it was nothing less than an emotional paddling. I returned to my seat accompanied by applause so perfunctory that it bordered on becoming a singular noun. It was a grim reminder that, as a comedian, you are naked on stage, laid bare to the whims of your crowd. You can clothe yourself in experience and self-assurance, but even then it can feel like you're prancing around in loose robes.

I had left Milton Keynes feeling like a king, turned up in Luton in the role of jester, and now I felt like a fool.

After twenty minutes, I said, 'It's been a pleasure talking to you, enjoy your evening,' left the stage area to unified booing (including the organiser) and didn't stop moving until I was halfway back to Manchester.

'Should've done the one about the Polish builders!' I heard before I passed out of the collective memory.

One person in Milton Keynes knew who I was. Three hundred people in Luton couldn't care less who I was.

Comedy.

**

There was also one person in Manchester who would now potentially boo me in public. The argument with Betty made me feel even worse about the horrendous gig, and the horrendous gig reciprocated.

I needed to redeem something, and I certainly wasn't going back to Luton, so I stopped at Toddington services on the M1 and tried to buy Betty some flowers. There weren't any, so I got her a neck pillow and a camping chair. They came to £30.45 (Battle of

Dingbat Mound).

Feeling totally wretched, I decided that a late-night Flat White and a tinkle would at least improve my physiological state, if not my emotional one.

There is a post-apocalyptic feel about service stations in the early hours that I like very much. I get a buzz from that sense of regal power that pulses through you when you walk into a deserted Men's Toilets and can take your pick from any of the hundred urinals. A few years ago, it became a bit of a game amongst some of the Manchester comedians to leave a packet of Monster Munch scrunched inside an empty bottle of Yopp by the sink of whichever service station you stopped at – as a sign to other members of the Order that you'd passed that way.

Where Gandalf used runes, we used calorific treats.

Back in Toddington, I chose a urinal with impunity and proceeded to go through the motions (pun intended). Seconds later, the sound of whistling from the entrance alerted me to another full-bladdered male in the vicinity. The echo of brogue on tile got louder...until the whistler stopped at the urinal next to me, halting me mid-flow.

Now, I don't really like being stood next to, trough-side, at the best of times (I always feel like people are trying to race me), but when you have ninety-nine urinals to choose from and you stand by the only other bloke in there, you are either sheltering for warmth or on a low-budget cruise. It was actually pretty mild out, so I narrowed those two options down fairly rapidly.

I was about to move away and finish my toilet in the safety of a lockable cubicle when this guy said 'Hey'. Not 'Hey' in a kind of 'How are you doing?' sort of way, but more in a kind of 'Hey, look at my penis' sort of way.

Impulsively, I looked across and found him presenting his schlong to me, as you might a commemorative sword.

What was happening? I expect this sort of behaviour at

Sandbach services, but not Toddington.

'Eeerrraagghh,' was roughly what I said by way of response.

What you need to know about me is that I'm not good at dealing with new situations. I panic. My mind is like an old sat nav on a new road (when it tries to tell you you're in a lake and should turn right in fifty yards along a road that isn't there). My mind is like that: it will take me down roads that aren't there. I love bantering and ad-libbing on-stage, but I've done it before and it doesn't throw me. Very rarely does something happen within the context of a gig that you couldn't anticipate after seven years of doing the job. In real life, lots of stuff happens that isn't feasible, and so I end up saying 'Eeerrraagghh' a lot.

Anyway, we now return to this guy, window-dressing his willy in front of me. And, y'know, credit where it's due: it was a monster. I don't condone sexual predatoriness of any kind, but you could at least see why he'd want to show it off. If I didn't know better, I'd say it had been CGI'd - although I don't think you'll see it on the new Disney Pixar. I hope not.

I had a number of options open to me. I could knock him spark out, make a break for it, sit him down in the camping chair and have a chat about boundaries. All perfectly justifiable. But I've told you I'm not good with new situations and so I did none of the above. What I did, instead, was applaud.

Not only was this the first applause I'd been privy to all night, but my spontaneous outburst was taken as positive feedback.

'Oh, thank you,' he said humbly. For one shreddingly surreal moment, I feared he was about to start an acceptance speech. This was getting worse by the moment, and yet still my brain refused to comply with my soul's desperate cry for help.

'So,' this guy said, buoyed by my inadvertent review, 'What do you think?'

At this point, I was like those contestants at the end of *Crystal*

Maze, frantically trying to grab an appropriate retort in the place of gold and silver tokens.

The first phrase that I managed to clasp in my metaphorical sweaty palm was: 'You should be very proud.' (If I was making this up, I'd use a phrase that made some kind of sense.)

'Are you interested then?' the Beastman furthered.

Fortunately, this is the exact same question asked by the German cannibal in an episode of *The IT Crowd* where he wants to eat Moss. My sat nav brain was out of the lake and back on to familiar territory.

'Oh no, it's not for me,' I confessed, quoting Moss verbatim.

Donkey Dong looked at me diffidently as I scuttled out of the Gents'. I wondered whether he might boo me as I left, but even heaving perverts, it seems, have more social grace than the audiences of corporate gigs. He even handed me the camping chair that was perched next to him when I awkwardly went back to reclaim it.

Even the most sordid of bucket-lists wouldn't include 'Getting propositioned by a man in polished brogues'. Still, these things can be formative. Certainly, if I ever revive the Monster Munch inside a Yopp thing, I might also start leaving a warning note.

I got back to the car and realised as I buckled up my seatbelt that I still hadn't finished my wee.

The next twenty miles were uncomfortable for a number of reasons, and despite the use of a new neck pillow.

**

If any of these 39 Steps was going to bring a sense of calm and equilibrium, it would surely be Oxford. And so it proved.

I was rostered to compere at Oxford Brookes Students' Union, with Joe Lycett, Andy White and Dan Logan bringing the funny alongside me. Florence the decrepit Fiesta carted me down to the shire mid-morning and I spent a few hours de-stressing around Blenheim Palace. Rumour has it that Winston Churchill was born in a ladies' toilet at Blenheim, although I would have happily swapped my own toilet misadventure for his. He was later quoted as saying, 'Although present on the occasion, I have no clear recollection of the event.' More recently, that is how I've come to view Willygate.

I had an early supper at the Eagle and Child pub in Oxford (where C.S. Lewis and J.R.R Tolkein used to meet) and used the opportunity to write up the Toddington story into a workable five minutes of material. The students loved it, and I left Oxford with an inkling of redemption. Oxford is perhaps the least dangerous place to which a young comedian can be sent.

Gig 12 of a possible 39 was in Lincolnshire, and was the result of a flurry of emails I'd sent out the day I got back from London and my meeting with Carlos. As soon as the County Challenge had been set, everyone in my Gmail address book had been politely spammed in search of work.
A woman whom I met once at a party or a rally or something slung back an email asking me to provide the entertainment for an event in Lincoln itself. I had stuck it in the diary as though my pen were a basilisk and the diary was Tom Riddle's diary. #notashamed

Betty had forgiven me for missing Marriage Prep, and I had forgiven her for saying hahahaha.ha down the phone when I rang to tell her about Luton. Only Betty had actually sought forgiveness on the matter, but we had agreed that the best prep for marriage was simply time together, and so she headed east with me.
'Do you like your new neck pillow, my lovely?'
'Yes, thanks. And you can never have too many camping chairs,

I always say. You must have put a lot of thought into those gifts.' She smiled askance and then leaned over to kiss me on the cheek...got restricted by her seat-belt and so kissed the part of my arm where I'd been injected against tuberculosis at age eleven.

A monsoon thrashed down all around us as Florence the crap Fiesta skidded to an abrupt halt in front of a ramshackle Community Centre. As we sprinted from the car to the entrance lobby, I employed a little technique I'd picked up on my travels for keeping the rain off: that of raising my right hand just over my head and using it as a shield. It did absolutely nothing.

'How long before someone mentions the phrase "Nice weather for ducks"?' Betty clamoured through the downpour.

'I give it a minute.'

I lost. It was sixteen seconds.

We tumbled into the lobby, shook ourselves caninely, frowned and exhaled quite a bit, then I said, 'Nice weather for ducks'. It was textbook coming-in-out-of-the-rain etiquette, and we'd nailed it.

'We're looking forward to seeing your big feet and silly hair,' chuckled the woman who greeted us.

Betty and I looked at each other sideways. This woman's ability to welcome newcomers hinted strongly at work experience with the UK Border Agency. #ididasatire #willigetintroubleforthat?

We were shown through to the auditorium (It was an auditorium in the same way that, as a kid, my Dad's back lawn was Wembley stadium). If you were going to base a gig's viability on attendees, it was perfectly sound – about eighty. But as I surveyed the wondrous crowd, my heart sank. Of that eighty, sixty of them were what scientists would call 'small children'. The other twenty were, as well.

'Oh, sugar my arse!' I thought, in my brain.

'Oh, sugar my arse!' I said out loud, using words.

'Is it all kids?' Betty asked nervously.

It did appear that way. There was a small chance that the audience was just much farther away than they looked, but I'd seen optical illusions before and this didn't feel right.

'Is everything all right?' asked the organiser, observing the whitening effect this view had had on my face.

'Yeah, u-huh, cool, absolutely, yeah, brill, no problem,' I said. It was classic realising-you-didn't-read-the-email-properly-and-not-wanting-to-show-your-fear etiquette, and I'd nailed it.

'Do you need a mirror to help you do your make-up?'

What was the matter with this woman? Why did she have to keep insulting me? What did she think I was, some kind of clow...oh no.

It was at this moment that the 'big feet and silly hair' comment uncloaked itself. Add the make-up comment into the mix, and it was obvious they were expecting a clown – well, that or a massive tranny, but that seemed unlikely given the demographic. Fear hit me in the face like hydrochloric acid squirted from a fake button-hole.

'Right, now, I'm probably not what you were expecting.' I used the word 'probably' in the same way the army uses the phrase 'Missing in Action'. It wasn't that I 'probably' wasn't a clown. I definitely wasn't.

'Look, I'm not a clown.' To date, that is the only time I've had to clear this up.

'But you are a children's entertainer, though, aren't you?'

Betty laughed.

I had once done some comedy workshops in a school, but they went apocalyptically badly and I spent most of the session being asked if I was gay, and told, in incrementally charming ways, that I had learning difficulties

'No, I'm not really a kid's entertainer...but my stuff is clean and upbeat and I'm here now, so let's just give it a go.'

'Have you got any popcorn?' Betty asked with a chuckle.

'Right kids, a bit of a surprise for you - we've got a stand-up comedian! Give a big cheer for Andy Kind!'

I went on and did my best. Most of the kids seemed to realise that I wasn't the clown they'd been promised. Some of them, sadly, didn't.

'He isn't dressed like a clown!'

'Where's his outfit?'

'Look at his silly red nose!'

I mined my own childhood archives for all the suitable jokes I could remember...which stretched to posing deep, philosophical questions about why poultry resolved to traverse a carriageway, and a handful of witty rejoinders about poo and wee.

'How long have I done?' I mouthed to Betty when I ran out of ideas.

'Two minutes,' she mouthed back between bites of popcorn.

Then someone shouted 'pile on', and fifty kids (and I think a couple of the supervisors) came charging at me, dragged me to the floor and erected a crude, human monument where I had once stood. It felt like a natural ending.

'Get off me. I want to go home. I think I've broken my ribs.'

Betty was trying to calm me down. I'd come off stage, having first being exhumed from the Andy Kind memorial statue, and my pride, spirit and kidneys were all hurting and bruised. I wanted to escape into the on-going monsoon and drop to my knees like Andy Dufresne.

'Look, at least go and say goodbye to the lady who booked you – it's rude to just go.'

'No, this is ridiculous – I can't keep turning up at die-on-your-arse events. Gigs that aren't gigs shouldn't be gigs!'

'But this is the price you pay for trying to fit thirty-nine gigs into ten weeks, my love – it's not going to get any easier.' She kissed me on my B.C.G arm again, and then on the cheek.

'Look, shall I get you a goody bag?'

'No. I mean yes. Then let's just go home. I just want to go home.'

I drove back west, munching on a Curly-Wurly and trying to work out which had been my favourite point of the week: the streetfight with Betty; being booed off in Luton; clapping a huge cock; or being beaten up by fans of *Waybuloo*. It was a tough one.

That weekend, I had a remarkably normal gig in Wiltshire, pre-booked before the 39 Steps began. It followed a comforting pattern: I drove to the gig, I did the gig, people laughed somewhat, I drove away from the gig.

It had still been a crap week. Comedy was my job – I wasn't used to such a high ratio of weird gigs to normals. But Betty was right. I was paying the price for taking whatever comedy scraps I could get. This wasn't any old run of gigs and, as Steve Martin said, 'With comedy, you have no place to go but more comedy, so you're never off the hook'.

To some degree, I was doing pretty well. I'd managed to complete fourteen of my 39 Steps in under a month, averaging a gig every other day. But I was already feeling the strain after the last four weeks, both on my performance as a comic on stage and my performance as a fiancée off it. Even with the valiant effort, the stark reality was that I was still under par, below average and off-track. My rampant, crazed ringing around had yielded some fruit, but some of it had turned sour (Lincolnshire), while some wasn't really fruit at all, but a gaping bum hole (Kent).

I was tired, away from Betty too much, I had lots of wedding stuff I hadn't done, and my diary was still too full of blankety blanks. It wasn't going well enough, as Carlos told me on the phone on the Sunday evening of T-Minus 7.

'It's not going well enough,' he said. I envisaged him in his London office, staring smugly at a framed portrait of himself.

'Besides,' Carlos continued, 'I'm not sure we want or need comedians who can't hold a crowd. Even if you do manage to do all these gigs - which I don't for a second believe that you will - then I will be the reluctantest of agents to take you on.

'To be fair, Carlos, a lot of these aren't normal gigs. I think I'm showing resolve and gumption by doing them at all.'

'And that's what I should tell promoters, is it? Book Andy Kind - he's great for any gig where he hand-picks the audience.'

'No...'

'Or how about this – "Do you want a comedian who will go on and plough through, despite a limited range? Then we've got just the man." And don't start about comedians specialising - you're not in the SAS. You're comedians - go on stage and be funny, then leave. No, you're going to have to take your ideas and upbuck them, and soon. Goodbye, Reggie!'

'Andy.'

I hated Carlos at that moment, and would continue to do so over the course of multiple ensuing moments.

'I wish I was in the SAS,' I said after the line went numb. 'You'd soon know about it. And reluctantest isn't a word.'

'Attaboy, Kindy. Why not say something mildly petulant after the conversation has finished? Take that, Carlos! You probably should be in the SAS with a ruthless streak like that.'

'Shut it, Horatio.'

(Horatio is the voice I give to my subconscious. He doesn't feature much here because I'm trying not to give him too much air time. I treat him like Russell Crowe treats Paul Bettany in the latter stages of *A Beautiful Mind* - I'm aware of his presence, but I just try to carry on as though I'm a normal person and I'm married to Jennifer Connelly.)

**

I was on house sitting duty for the evening. Grandad was taking my Gran to a Tea Dance and they couldn't possibly leave the house unattended, in case it got burgled and the thieves got away with all the

VHS cassettes and that little carriage clock on the mantlepiece with the swinging pendulum.

I could hear Grandad coughing his way to the front door long before he opened it. He stood there, resplendent in his best/only suit and war medals.

'Thanks for coming over, son. I never feel comfortable leaving the place unattended – you never know who's watching.'

What you did know, actually, was that the area in which Gran and Grandad lived was one of the most affluent and unthreatened in the region. There were gangs on the prowl, but they tended to diss you with rhyming couplets and rumble with art.

Grandad was clearly excited about a rare trip out, because he repeatedly checked himself over in the full-length hall mirror.

'Not too shabby…not too shabby at all. She wants me to wear a flower, but I told her, I'm not a clown. Shouldn't really have to inform her of that after so many years.'

'I think you look great!' I chimed.

'Help yourself to what you want from the pantry – there's plenty of Monster Munch, and some of that yoghurt drink you like in the fridge. We're going to the place we first met tonight. She's just upstairs, sorting out her lipstick.'

'I hope you have a lovely time, both of you.'

'Well, we will if she would hurry up a bit?!' He shouted this last part up the stairs, then started coughing again.

'Never once has she been early for anything, your Gran. Still, she's a good'un. She drives me up the wall, but she's a good'un.'

T-Minus 6 Weeks

"After all, damn it, what does being in love mean if you can't trust a person?"
Evelyn Waugh

It was my parents' wedding anniversary, and all the family had gathered at Mum and Dad's house to celebrate.

My sister Jen had informed me of this special occasion the day before (The retention of it had been ejected from my own mind by the knowledge that Reading has a massive stone lion). I don't think my parents guessed at my lapse, though - after all, nothing says 'Happy 30th Wedding Anniversary' better than a bumper pack of Jelly Babies and some cheese.

Nevertheless, it was nice to be back at Kind Towers. A massive homemade carvery was followed by a massive trifle, after which I decided on a massive nap in front of *Deal or No Deal*. That's the kind of non-comformist hotshot you're dealing with here, gentle reader. I don't wish to scare you, but I will regularly remove a memory stick before it's safe to do so.

Post-meat, Betty and Mum repaired to the conservatory and started nattering about seating plans and heart-shaped balloons. Invited guests had started to R.S.V.P with polite declines, and with each rejection the catering bill dropped and I got closer and closer to affording a wedding suit (if I ever got round to ordering it). We still needed more drop-outs, to keep me from bankruptcy and outright liquidation, but quite a few invitees had withdrawn once they realised, happily, that they didn't like us as much as they liked a free Saturday.

Following G-reg's dumping by his horrendous girlfriend - and her subsequent extraction - Victor Smithers had suggested trying to break up other relationships by sending him in as an evil love guru. I politely declined and he called me a paedophile.

As the other women gleefully debated what shade and texture of ribbon would be most salubrious, my sister Jenny joined me in the living room for nap time. We stretched out on separate sofas and skyplussed '*Deal*' - the show that is, essentially, a long-winded advent calendar.

I love a nap. I wasn't going to tell you initially (some people are a bit sceptical about adults who nap), but I don't care. Everything about a nap is incredible, and it's perhaps the single best thing about being a comedian. While the fools and horses are slaving away into a weekday afternoon, I'm at home, dreaming about being a wizard. The only downside to napping, in fact, is that twenty-second period as you're waking when fantasy and reality blur and you realise, with much despondency, that you're not really a wizard at all.

When I woke from my slumber, *Deal* was still on, but Jenny was sitting bolt upright on her sofa, looking excited.
'I think I might be pregnant,' she said from nowhere.
'Well, Noel is very charismatic – you're only a woman after all,' I responded drowsily.
'No, seriously Andy, it's just hit me – I think I'm pregnant.'
Was this real, or was I still napping? I checked to see if I was a wizard. No, damn, it was real.
This was a new situation for me, and so sat nav brain duly kicked in and I reacted like the flailing ignoramus that I am.
'Right, OK...er...right, you stay there, I'll get you a bowl of cold water and some hot towels.'
'What are you talking about?' my sister asked, treating my ignorance with the scorn it surely merited. 'I don't mean I'm

having a baby now. I just think that...surely you know how pregnancy works, don't you?'

'Sorry, I got confused and went on instinct.'

'Not a very good instinct, though. You went to get a bowl of cold water and hot towels – you've confused delivering a baby with ordering Chinese food.'

I had done just that, in fact.

'So, how do you know you're pregnant, then? Are you craving something? I fancy some Chinese food – we could get takeaway?'

'No, I'm not hungry – I just feel it, I think. I can't be sure, but this could be it.'

A wizard would have known exactly what to do here. I hated not being a wizard.

Abruptly, a half-tattered memory staggered out of my subconscious.

'We could do an online pregnancy test!' I exclaimed, confidently. I'd read something in a magazine once, and so it must be accurate.

'An online pregnancy test? I don't think that's possible, bro. Certainly not here anyway – Dad's computer isn't even touch-screen.'

What I had half-remembered, and what I would have said (had I not been weighing up the contrasting merits of Hoi Sin Duck vs Sweet'n'Sour Chicken) was an online survey. Having only half-remembered reading about them, I had forgotten the half where it stated, quite clearly, that online surveys to verify pregnancy were absolute balderpiffle.

However, within minutes – and wanting to be the helpful older brother – we had askjeevesed our way to a survey entitled 'The 10 signs that you might be pregnant'.

Settling down next to my sister, we worked our way through a series of ten scholarly, scientific questions designed to ascertain pregnancy. Questions like 'Have you put on weight?', 'Are you experiencing mood swings?' and, most clinically, 'Are parts of your body hairier than they used to be?'

Out of ten questions, Jenny answered 'Yes' to seven, which gave her a reasonable impression that she might be pregnant. I, on the other hand, answered 'Yes' to all ten questions – leaving me in no doubt that I was, miraculously, with child.

Question 9 was the clincher: 'Have you missed your period?'

'Well, I'm still waiting...oh no!'

'What are you doing?' Betty asked as she brought in a tray of teas.

'I'm going to have a baby,' we both said.

**

I had four dates with Old Lady Stand-up in the diary for T-Minus 6. The halfway point was approaching and, if the score stayed the same, I would be two gigs behind schedule. To encourage me, Carlos sent me a Youtube clip with chipmunks being blown apart by shotguns.

I manned the phone for hours on end, cold-calling industry bods in search of gigs. To no avail - the promoters weren't budging.

'Sorry, mate – we're booked up until the new year.' (Essex)

'You've played here within the last year, fella – no can do.' (Derbyshire)

'I don't rate you as a comic. Please don't call again.' (Numerous)

The X-Factory of the age had asphyxiated the comedy circuit and meant that hundreds of comics were applying for each morsel of stage time. My incessant barrage of calls, texts and singing pleadograms *had* secured me a handful of gigs, but I was starting to antagonise people with my constant pestering. Worse, the gigs I was being offered were, as often as not, outside the parameters of Carlos' Commandments - either in counties I'd already vanquished or disabled in some other way.

'We don't have a budget, mate, but we can pay you in beer,' one geezer from London chimed down the phone.

'Thanks - that will make the four-hour journey back fun. I'll leave it.'

I was hanging in there (like that famous poster of the cat clinging to the washing line), but I couldn't allow for any more setbacks. And I still knew nothing about the whereabouts of flipping Rutland.

At least I attended Marriage Prep for the first time, cancelling a gig in Stoke to be there. Traditionally, I'd treated gigs like Francis of Assisi treated animals – by welcoming all-comers. Now I was more like a burly, belligerent door-supervisor: if your name's not down on the Euro 96 wall chart, you're not coming in (the diary).

There were six couples on the Marriage prep course. Betty and I were the only greenhorns, and so the leader (a guy named Clive who'd just recovered from SARS) ran us cursorily through the premise.

'We've already covered some of the basics, guys, but it's stuff that you should already know, hopefully,' he chuckled, 'like sharing out chores and remembering not to hit each other.'

We were new, and I hadn't got to the point where I said I was a comedian, so five other couples looked on aghast as I noted down 'Don't strike her' and then declared, 'I'm learning!' A timely reminder that jokes don't work out of context. #comedywriting101

'Tonight,' the former pneumonee continued, 'we're going to be looking at how we prioritise our partner in the relationship – learning to put each other first.'

Betty looked across at me and smiled with mock innocence. I made a mental note to strike her.

'Thanks for coming, honey – I really appreciate it,' Betty chirped as we drove home.

'Well, it was better than contracting SARS.'

'I'm glad you see it that way. And I can't wait to spend my birthday with you on Sunday.'

'Yes, I have a nice surprise planned for you.'

'Oooooh,' she ooooohed.

'What the hell was that sound?'

She giggled and punched me playfully on the arm.

'Hey, you're not allowed to do that – Clive said!'

There would actually be two surprises for Betty's birthday, but only one of them was advertent. Still, let's leave it on a high for now, shall we?

**

For the first gig of the week, I drove to Gillingham. That's right, Gillingham. Not to be confused with Gillingham, which is in a totally different county. Luckily for me I got to see both of them because, when you confirm gigs via email, how could you possibly know that the woman meant Gillingham and not Gillingham? You couldn't and I didn't. So for the second time in a month, I drove to Kent in search of giggles, and left gigless. Gillingham in Dorset plated up a lovely gig, but I'd already tucked into Dorset during this thirty-nine-course challenge and so it was pointless. I drove home feeling like I'd bitten into a Heston Blumenthal steak in the shape of a Claymore, only to realise that it was a live Claymore. Kent was clearly an idiot. I mean, I regularly did six stupid things before breakfast, but this was ridiculous.

And so to Cheshire. The next gig on the Andy Kind Caravan of Disaster was at Alexander's in Chester.

The Romans settled Chester in…er…Roman times, and called it Deva Victrix (which I'm fairly sure was the name of one of the

Death-eaters in *Harry Potter*). The conurbation has been there for many moons, and so suitably, Alexander's is the longest-running comedy club outside London, having been operational for over two decades. It's a good venue and, better still, it was fifty minutes from my house, qualifying it as a local gig!

Unequivocally for comedians, any journey less than an hour is practically 'round the corner'. The nub of the job might be stage-time, but the majority of our time is spent hauling ass – to the point where we feel more like same-day couriers delivering jokes.

The downside to gigging at Alexander's is that, whereas most gigs bully off around 8:00pm, show time here is 9.30pm. The audience has been in there since about 7.30pm, eating and getting hammers (That should read 'hammered' – oh well, too late to change it now). So by the time the punters even set eyes on a comedian, those eyes are blurry and looking around for a karaoke machine.

The other odd thing is that there is no compere. Now, they've been running comedy since I was ten, so I'm in no position to criticise their position, but this bit flummoxes me. With any crowd, but especially one drinking to such Viking proportions, you need someone who can go on, soak up excess chatter like a talkative sponge, lather the audience up, and then bring on the acts to hose them down. This is what a compere does. On every occasion I've played Alexander's, I've always left thinking, 'They should have had a compere...and fewer hammers.'

Most of the 39 Steps I'd climbed so far had been one-man shows, and so it was healthy to have other comics on the bill to chat to - and to gang up with if some toddlers tried a pile-on. My old mate Sam Avery and TV-funnyman-Nathan-Caton were attendant that night. We sat at the back prior to show time, nomming on free burgers, and they both asked me how the challenge was going.

'It's going...but I'm not sure in what direction,' I replied with almost Wildean poise, then choked on a gherkin.

I got on stage for my bit about 10.15pm, by which time the audience was like a scene from Odin's feasting hall. I commenced, in the absence of a compere, by bantering with the assembled mass of drukkenskab (the Danish word for 'drunkenness', that I learnt the hard way during a corporate in Copenhagen).

The bavardage was going very well, but the problem came when I started rolling out my material. The drukkens in the crowd struggled to comprehend that the interaction had stopped and refused to relax their shield-wall of obtuse heckling.

'Why would anyone marry you, slaphead?'

'I'm going to the bar – you want anything?'

'Has anyone seen my hammer?'

I managed to placate most of them, but one (a rubbery, flubbery bloke who looked like a Mr. Man) decided to prolong the heckling battle after his fellow kinsmen had retreated.

Now, listen in. Heckles, and the hecklers who vomit them out, are generally pigswill. In comedy mythology, the heckler is the nemesis of the comedian: a sinuous, elusive creature that stalks the clubs, preying on unsuspecting comics with adroit wordplay. In reality, the heckler is a drunken pillock who brings a wooden sword to a gunfight.

Hecklers almost always lose. A heckle stems from a compound assumption in the mind of the heckler – both parts of which are usually misinformed. First, that the heckler is funny. Second, that the comic on stage is not.

Forgive me for my tribal nepotism here, but with very limited exceptions, you (the audience) are not as funny as us (the comedians). That's why, when the organisers start to book the night, we get the phone call.

I've maybe heard ten genuinely good heckles in seven years (I may have heard one in Copenhagen, but it was in Danish, so who knows?) Perhaps three of these left the comic speechless. Even if the comic isn't sharp enough to infuse the moment with adept spontaneity, s/he has a full arsenal of archived put-downs, passed down from generation to generation of comics.

All told, it's not a high hit-rate with heckling, and while muggles might think that hecklers are the comic's single greatest fear, they scare us about as much as Keats would be scared taking on a mute in a poetry slam.

In short, then, if you are considering heckling, remember this: you am not legend.

I've only once been totally destroyed by a heckle. This wasn't it. Stay tuned.

When crossing swords with the *Hecklus Drunkenus Genus*, the major obstacle is that they don't have enough remaining brain cells to process their defeat, and will often plough on with their mouthfarts long after their wooden swords have been obliterated.

I used a stray hammer to nail the gig, and the majority of Norsemen gave me a nice big pillagey cheer as I squeezed off stage. I would be home within an hour – and then up early to cook Betty a birthday breakfast.

I was bidding farewell to my old mate Sam Avery and TV-Funnyman-Nathan-Caton, packing up my note-pad and pen, when we were interrupted by The Heckler, flubbering over to remonstrate with me.

'If you don't want people to interact, don't interact!' he bellowed at me, a vein rearing up in his temple. It would have been a reasonable point, if he hadn't missed the actual point. I tried to explain to him that interaction was fine, but that the crowd was paying to listen to me, not him. #comedyclubhousekeeping101

At this point, several other veins manifested themselves on The

Heckler's skull. He yanked the pen out of my hand and hurled it backwards, then waggled his finger about an inch from my face, telling me that he had paid good money to be there – presumably, meaning that he could therefore ruin the show for others if he chose.

Now, I'm not a violent man. Indeed, I like to think of myself as a peacemaker (NB. I also like to think of myself as the rightful successor to the Batman cowl, so thoughts in themselves are no gauge of accuracy). I gently put a calming hand on The Heckler's shoulder. He reacted as anyone would in that situation, by falling to the ground clutching his face.

'What the…?' I looked over at Sam and TV-Funnyman-Nathan-Caton. They both wore looks that said, 'What the…?'

The Heckler – a man in his late forties in a Burton's suit - starting rolling around on the floor and screaming, attracting the attention of everyone else in the venue.

'The comedian just smacked that heckler,' one person said.

'Good,' someone else said.

The Heckler's two mates came piling over, as did the venue manager.

'Come on then, mate – let's go!' growled his mates, primordially.

'What the hell is going on?' asked the manager.

The Heckler stopped rolling around instantly and rose to his knees, pointing at me with incredulity on his lying face. There was then a time/space vortex thing where he turned into a seven-year-old child.

'He hit me!'

'Hit you?!' the manager gasped.

'Really hard in the face!'

'What are you talking about? I didn't touch you!' I protested, my voice nuzzling the sound barrier.

I was apparently globe-trotting my way through the evening.

Having been heckled by 9th Century Scandinavians, I had now stumbled, seemingly, into a game from the Copa America.

'He didn't hit you, fella,' my old mate Sam Avery averred.

At this, Hecklinho and his two mates surrounded the female venue manager, as though she had disallowed a perfectly good goal they had just scored – which she hadn't. What was this guy doing? Was he hoping I'd get sent off and banned for three matches.

'Did you hit him?' one punter asked me with a grin.

'No.'

'Want *me* to?'

'No, thanks.'

Hecklinho refused to back down and worked himself up into delirium.

'I want him sacked from working here!'

'He doesn't work here – he's just finished.' The venue manager was infinitely more patient than me, and exemplary in her professionalism.

'Then I want him arrested!'

I don't wish to be cynical, but it's almost as though those 'Drink Responsibly' warnings don't work.

This was Chester city centre on a weekend, and so within minutes a brace of coppers was on the scene. They took the two of us outside and sat us on a wall for questioning. This was ridiculous. The rest of the audience went back inside to watch TV-Funnyman-Nathan-Caton headline the show. Nathan had been given his TV break on *Mock the Week*. Mine would come, seemingly, on *BBC News24* (In fact, it would come a few months later on *Songs of Praise*. #check #me #out)

The truth was quickly established through eye-witness testimony, the fact that The Heckler's face bore no marks whatsoever, and the fact that his pants were on fire. The police apologised to me and warned the middle-aged interloper for breach of the peace. I went back inside to look for my stray pen, but it had been snaffled as plunder.

I collapsed into bed at 1:00am. So much for getting home within an hour. The gig itself had gone well, but my patience was raggedy, my comedy enjoyment levels running on fumes, and I'd nearly been arrested for a crime I didn't commit.

'Still,' I mused, as my eye-lids got heavier, 'that means I'm only one step away from being the A-Team...you know what, yes - I *am* like the A-Team.'

Copa America Semi-Final:
Heckler 0 Kindy 1
                Missed pen
(Kindy through to play Brazil in the Final).

**

Betty's birthday dawned and, although shattered from my confab with the diva from Deva, I was round at hers by 8:30am to knock-up a surprise breakfast – which had stopped being a surprise the moment she opened her door and I said, 'I'm here to cook you some breakfast.'

Scrambled eggs, sausages, bacon, fried tomatoes, hash browns, mushrooms: I'd forgotten to buy all of it (Told you: six stupid things before breakfast).

'Right, well, you can either have toast with a choice of butter or...no butter, or I can take you out for breakfast.'

'Take me out for lunch, honey – toast will be fine for now.'

'Would you like some butter with that?'

'Yes, please!'

I had bought Betty a number of gifts. That number was one, but it was a good one. I had commissioned an artist to paint the two of us in full wedding regalia against the backdrop of St. John's

Church, Duxford, Cambridgeshire – where we would soon be married. Tears filled her eyes as she unwrapped it, and it wasn't until later that she told me my waistcoat on the painting would clash with the bridesmaids' dresses and I would have to change it.

Betty loved the painting, though, and wanted to see it hanging on the wall that morning. So like a good husband-to-be, I went to the local hardware shop, bought the relevant bits and bobs, then made a total hash of it and almost knocked a wall through. Betty cried again and I called my Dad, who drove all the way from Stoke-on-Trent to put up a picture and call me a moron (The latter was, in fact, the reason he agreed to the former).

As Dad dealt with the path of destruction I had trailed at Betty's house, I took milady for a slap-up meal at the local Comfort Day Lodge Travel Inn or something. #youstayclassyandykind

The musk of a thousand broken Valentine's Day dreams filled our nostrils as we entered the hotel eaterie.

'I'll do something nice for your thirtieth,' I rerereiterated to Betty.

'Don't worry, honey. I know you've had a difficult last few...life.' She held my hand and impersonated someone having a lovely birthday. 'The fact that you're here is the most important.'

The young lad who showed us to our table was new.

'I'll be serving you today – my name is...' At this moment he pointed to a badge on his shirt that read, 'If I don't tell you about our Breakfast, have one on us for free!'

'That's a bit of a weird name,' I joked (It's jokes like that that got me *Songs of Praise*, ya'll).

'Oh, whoops,' he chuckled, and then pointed to another badge that said 'Richard'.

I didn't give it much thought initially. After all, with a badge that says 'If I don't tell you about our breakfast, have one on us for free' displayed on your shirt, you're not going to forget to tell people about breakfast, are you...Richard?

And yet Richard was new. His confusion as to whether his name was Richard or If-I-don't-tell-you-about-our-breakfast-have-one-on-us-for-free, highlighted his total ineptitude to do what is quite frankly a very simple job.

He brought our starters, and he said nothing about breakfast. He brought our main courses, got them totally wrong, went back, dropped a plate of Chicken Satay skewers, came back with the right mains, and he said nothing about the breakfast. He replenished our drinks, not once, not twice, but thrice, and he said nothing about the breakfast.

We got to the end of dessert and asked for the bill, and still Richard had singularly failed to say anything about breakfast.

'I'm just gonna go for it,' I asserted to Betty.

'You're a maverick and my absolute hero,' she has never said.

'Thanks, guys,' Richard said as he placed the small plate of change on our table.

'Richard?!' I said, emphatically. I had meant to say his name in the way you might if you were playing hide-and-seek and you knew he was hiding behind the settee. Instead, I said it in the way you might if you'd just found out he was the mastermind behind an evil terrorist plot that you'd been working alongside MI6 to crack for a number of years.

'Yes?' Richard responded.

'...You failed to tell us about breakfast, and now we want a free one.'

Richard's face dropped like an outdated reference to interest rates. We had him and he knew it.

'Right,' he gulped. 'You'll have to speak to my boss about that, then...'

'Great, I will,' I barked triumphantly, making for the bar.

'Please don't!' Richard yelped like a dog who had seen interest rates on its ISA drop dramatically.

The colour drained from Richard's face as he continued his plea.

'Please don't say anything, sir. I've only been here a week and I'm already on a final warning. This could mean the end for me...'

I'm not sure I've ever felt more torn in my life. I was one complaint away from securing every British man's dream: a complimentary fry-up. But it would mean the whimpering end to a short-lived career for the oft-mentioned Richard.

While pondering my recourse, a singular thought struck me: this badge Richard wore was totally misrepresentative of his situation. What the badge really should have said was 'If I don't tell you about our breakfast, I will be severely reprimanded and instantly fired from my job working here'. Maybe they just couldn't find a badge big enough to fit all that on, or maybe they realised that the truth was a little bit too third-reichy to attract customers.

'We won't say anything,' Betty insisted as Richard's eyes filled with tears. She shot me another one of those looks that would soon be termed 'wifey'.

'Tell me more about this breakfast,' I demanded, unwilling to yield.

'Well,' he spluttered, 'It's eggs – scrambled or poached – bacon, sausages...'

'...How many sausages?'

'…three sausages...tomato, mushrooms...'

At this point the Bar Manager strode over, alerted by Richard's tears.

'What's going on here?!'

It was the second time in just over twelve hours that a venue manager had needed to intervene in my life.

Betty and Richard both looked at me with deep, visceral pleading in their eyes. #wwjd?

'......Richard here was just telling us about your breakfast,' I said flatly.

Richard gazed at me in wonder. I had given him a glimmer of

hope - like a scene without Ben Affleck in a film starring Ben Affleck.

'Well, why are you crying, Richard?' asked his boss.

Now, to be fair to Richard, I never thought he had this in him, but credit where it's due – he nailed it.

'Well...,' he began, his life-force returning, '...it's just such a good deal. I always well up.'

Well played, sir.

'Excellent!' erupted the Bar Manager, turning on his heel and bustling off.

'Here, have this.' Richard spoke earnestly as he handed over the badge that said, "If I don't tell you about our breakfast, have one on us for free". 'Please, take it, as a sign of my gratitude.'

'You could always just give me £7.99 in cash for a breakfast,' I shot back (Yes, I think that *is* what Jesus would have done).

Betty patted my hand and led me solemnly away.

**

We got back to Betty's house as Dad was finishing off, having replastered part of a wall and hung up the painting. I was wearing my new badge like a medal of honour.

'I can have a quick cup of tea, and then I need to head off, too,' I said, hoving in for a cuddle.

'Pardon?' Betty's face dropped as she Brianodriscolled.

'I'm in Northants tonight, gigging. You knew that, didn't you?'

'No, I didn't. Why have you taken a gig on my birthday?'

'Flippin'eck, not this again, lovely. I've told you, I can't pick and choose dates – I don't decide what day the gig is on, do I? The Gods of Comedy do that.'

'But it's my birthday – I wanted to spend it with you.'

'And you have. I've bought you lunch...and I put a lot of thought into that gift – although you seem more concerned about the colour of the flipping waistcoat!' (I'm not toning down here – I do frequent the word flipping.)

Betty slumped into a chair and her eyes watered up again. Abruptly, she shot back up and let loose.

'Is this what it's going to be like, Andy? All our lives, quality time together cut short 'cos you've got to go and make strangers laugh?!'

'What?'

'I love the gift you got me, and lunch – but it's quality time with my husband I want. It just feels at the moment that, even when you're here, you're not really here. You're never fully present.'

'I've said sor…'

'You haven't said sorry!! Stop saying you've said sorry when it's blatantly obvious to everyone else in the room that you haven't said sorry!!'

'I'll go, shall I?' asked Dad.

'Please.'

'OK. Can you tell me about the breakfast?'

'Later.'

Dad shuffled out.

'Look, Betts, I am sorry…I'm sorry that you don't want to support me in this challenge. I've been doing it for us, so I could give us a good start in married life, but all you do is complain about me being away all the time. I am a *comedian*. That is what I do – I comede…I do comedy, I mean.'

My heart was starting to descend through my body, passing the rising anger on the stairs.

'And what if I asked you to stop – to give it up for me?' Betty's eyes were translucent with tears now.

I stared blankly at the painting of two happily married people, and said nothing.

'You see? You claim to be doing this challenge for me, but you're not, you're doing it for you – for your own glory! Well, go on, then – off you go and do your precious comedy. I'll be fine here on my own!'

'Happy Birthday,' I said, storming out of the house. I heard heavy exhalations before I slammed the door. Betty was either sobbing hard or inflating a dingy. I didn't go back to check.

I drove away furious. They say that comedy is a young, single man's game. I was starting to understand what that meant.

In my opinion - an opinion I respect, and I think we all should - Betty was being totally unreasonable. I didn't want to see her cry (it made me want to cry), but she seemed to be creating an unfair ultimatum between herself and comedy. What was she expecting me to do once we got married? Become a vicar?! No chance.

For the first time since I met Betty, I started worrying about giving up the single life. From the moment I'd met her, I'd been planning our life together, thinking how fantastic it would be to get married and live happily ever after as comedian and wife. At no point had I thought that my young wife and Old Lady Stand-up wouldn't get on.

The life of a single comic is great. You get up when you want, start writing when (if) you want, eat what you want, nap and dream of wizarding. Sometimes I would set my alarm for 6:45am, wake up like all the people with normal jobs...then give the clock the Vs and go back to sleep for another three hours.

As a single comic, if you want to spend an entire day sitting in your pants, drinking pop and bidding online for cattle, you can. There's no hierarchy, no dissenters. You are the despot of your own little world.

Moderation doesn't work in comedy. You can't do the job unless you are somehow out of step with the rest of society - unless you inhabit the grey areas between black and white. Like a ska band, you play on the off-beat.

But that would all change once (if) I got married.

Marriage is based on self-sacrifice. It's about putting your old single self to death. From the moment you say 'I do', you no longer exist in isolation: you become one half of a new creation. Within this new creation you give yourself fully to your spouse, forsaking all others – including your old self.

But as I seethed my way back to the flat, I wasn't interested in forsaking the old Andy Kind. I saw my single self standing on the executioner's scaffold, the noose being tightened round his neck. And I wanted to cry out. I didn't want him to die.

I didn't want to stop coming home after a gig and lying in bed with a kebab and *Thundercats* on DVD (even if it did too often lead to scary dreams about Mumm-Ra or erotic ones about Cheetarah). I didn't want to prioritise rinsing the pans over rinsing a gig. I didn't want to stop doing comedy because of someone else's small-mindedness.

Comedy had been my first love, and I loved her still.

I started considering that maybe Betty and I weren't right for each other after all. Maybe she needed someone more mature, someone more malleable? She was a campaigner - her *raison d'etre* was fighting for the rights of the stifled voices in society. My *raison d'etre* was hiding behind doors and jumping out at people.

I reflected, as I ignored the big pile of washing up and the sex sounds coming from Pob's room, that the birthday painting on Betty's wall might not need altering in the colour of the waistcoat. It might need a different face.

**

I want to apologise for using the phrase *raison d'etre* just now. I don't get much occasion to use my French degree these days, and so peppering the odd sentence with *un petit peu de francais* makes me feel like those four years and forty thousand pounds weren't wasted. Thanks for understanding.

The English language is a language of immigrants. Though it remains the most spoken and most revered language in the world, all the words which we might think of as quintessentially English have been imported from overseas at some point. It is something of a curio, then, that in recent times the English language has become reflective of the English people: wary of outsiders. The French language is always happy to integrate foreigners into its midst: *l'internet, le Big Mac*, and, should you want to purchase a Phil Collins anthology, *le Best Of* – amongst others. This is in stark contrast with English, which looks down on anything too namby pamby and continental (Have you ever tried using the phrase *le mot juste* in a pub and been allowed to stay?)

Latin is an exception to the rule. Using Latin makes you seem intelligent. Ergo, it can be used ad infinitum and help one maintain a certain *je ne sais quoi* – no, you see, I've ruined it. Q.E.D.

My point is that we need a few new recruits. For instance, there isn't a word in the mother tongue to sum up the feeling you get when you arrive at a car park one minute after the charging period elapses. Jubilation, you might propose? And I considered that, but no. It's more like one tsp jubilation, a pinch of pleasant surprise and a great big calorific dollop of sticking it to the man.

More pertinently, I've looked everywhere and we still don't have a single, concise word for that scenario whereby you travel for ages through rush-hour traffic, arrive at your destination - which happens to be at the other end of the country - only to find that the reason for your entire visit doesn't exist. There are words that we use in that scenario, but they tend to get replaced by asterisks and pound signs in stories like this.

'Have you heard from the promoter?' Victor Smithers enquired of Vince Atta as we chugged down the M6 towards

Northampton (Victor was supposed to be driving, but his frozen hand had flared up again, while I was feeling about as stable as Patrick Bateman in the latter stages of *American Psycho*, so Vince was at the wheel).

'Not today, no, but he called a few days ago. I'm sure everything's fine.'

'What's wrong with you, Kindy?' Victor asked with derision.

The gruelling four-hour drive, in which our only company was a desultory game of *Boat, Bike, Honk*, had been worsened by a call from the promoter for the next day's gig - in Romford, Essex. This guy sheepishly confessed that they hadn't managed to sell enough tickets at such short notice, and could they cancel and re-book me after my honeymoon? I thanked the guy for trying to help me out, then emitted asterisks and pound signs out of the window.

My gig count for T-Minus 6 was now two – half of what I needed to stop falling further behind my already lagging tally. I pictured the poster of the cat hanging by its paw to the washing line...and imagined it being speared through the spine (after which it would plummet to its doom, but it would be dead before it hit the ground).

I'd realised that Betty was partly right about the 39 Steps: I wasn't doing it for her. In truth, I wasn't really pursuing it for any motive other than sheer pig-headedness.

I didn't want Carlos as my agent – I thought he was a pompous, vainglorious dckihaed. And the growing enmity between us made the idea of representation laughable. But I hated being told I couldn't or wouldn't do something. I just wanted to beat him.

Throughout my life, people had told me to stop daydreaming about becoming a comedian - that I should just get a proper job. I'd scrimped and saved and dug deep and broken my nose on the grindstone, but I'd shown them they were wrong. And all my energy, all my will, was now being ploughed into showing Carlos the same thing. He had appropriated the faces of all those historic doubters from school and university. He had come to symbolise all of them. He *was* all of them.

I was steadily losing the joy of doing stand-up comedy. But the will to do it, to show that I wasn't a fraud, was stronger than ever. My defiance was carrying me on as if by gravitation.

Vince found the venue and called Victor and me over.

'A bit quiet,' Smithers mused.

'Yeah, and that's why, fellas,' Vince groaned, pointing to a big black A-board with the chalky words: 'Comedy tonite, Cancelled due to unforeseen circs'...at which point the person had run out of board.

'Is this a joke?' Victor asked without mirth.

In any situation, when a comedian has to ask another comedian whether something is intended as humour, you know it's a dead-end.

We paced into the venue, brows furrowing and jaws setting in the evolutionary way that says, quite simply, 'Danger.' There was a couple of blokes perched at the bar, wearing dungarees and covered in paint. I presume they were decorators, but they could have been renegade urban paintballers - I was too concerned to enquire.

'Excuse me, pal,' Victor called to the scrawny barman, who didn't look old enough to drink coffee, let alone beer. He did, however, look like he'd very recently discovered marijuana.

'We're comedians for tonight. We've come down from Manchester and we've not heard anything about a cancellation. What's going on?'

'It's cancelled, mate,' answered Harry Pothead.

'BUT WHY IS IT CANCELLED??!!!' Rage took me, giving voice to that emotion which, if only we had a word for it, would have slotted in cosily here.

'Chill out, dude,' said one of the paintballing decorators, giving himself away as the wacky-backy trader.

'I'll chill out when someone tells me why the gig has been cancelled!' I was snarling in that evolutionary way that says... well, you know what a snarl means.

Neither the manchild behind the bar nor the hippy painters was going to tell us anything useful, so Vince set barboy to work getting us a round of cokes, and I went to call the promoter.

'Hello, mate!' he answered with unwise urbanity, as though we were going on holiday together.

'We're at the venue. You aren't at the venue. Why aren't you at the venue?'

'Oh, did you guys not get my text?'

There have been some abysmal excuses since God invented the larynx (I didn't realize the knife was sharp; I wasn't groping – it was a tickle fight; we thought we'd signed John Barnes, not Luther Blissett), but there can be few more pallid, more loathsome excuses than 'Did you not get my text?'

'Massive sorries,' the promoter said, without feeling.

'*&£$%£%&**' I replied, with it. Unable to do anything as satisfying as slam the phone down, I angrily pressed the bit of glass that said 'End Call' and stalked back inside.

'Kindy, do you fancy sharing a pizza with these guys?' Victor asked, holding something illegal in his right hand.

'No. I'm going home. I just want to go home. I need to return some video tapes.'

The evening was like a bad joke – a long journey with no pay off. And I was the butt of it.

We left feeling dismal. Vince cheered me up briefly, by rubbing out the chalk on the A-board and replacing it with "Attention Police: illegal substances inside".

Paintball your way out of that one, 'dude'.

By the time I got home, I couldn't even drum up enough

enthusiasm for *Thundercats*. I was under the distinct impression that both the ladies in my life were wilfully undermining my teetering masculinity. Betty didn't want me canoodling with comedy, and when I left her on her birthday to go and do comedy, comedy stood me up.

I'd done one gig this week. One. I needed to do four and I'd done one. The word 'Cheshire' sat there in the weekly update to Carlos, looking how I felt: lonely. And on its own.

Carlos, in his reply to my dutiful email, included a pic of The Cheshire Cat from *Alice in Wonderland*, its inhospitable smile hung across its face - spearing me through the spine.

The life of a single comic is shit.

**

'What have you done with all the sausages?!'
Gran was on the warpath.
The sausages, I knew, had been fried in butter and eaten with bacon, cooked tomatoes and several rounds of white bread. It was quite a breakfast.
Gran flung open the door and stared menacingly down at her husband.
'We ate them, my love. Andrew's a growing lad.'
'Growing outwards like you if you're not careful. And those sausages were for a casserole tonight,'
Grandad got gingerly to his feet and hoved towards Gran for a cuddle. Gran sidestepped.
'Oi – why have you Jeremyguscotted me?'
'Because you're annoying – and you haven't washed up. This marriage won't work if it's me doing everything.'
Grandad guffawed without mockery. He placed his hand gently on Gran's shoulder and turned her towards a painting on the wall.
'Look at that – do you see that? That's us on our wedding day, that is - nearly fifty years ago. Had it painted specially, didn't I?'

'You did.'

'Yes, all told, I think we've done a pretty good job of being married, don't you?'

'It doesn't mean you can eat all my sausages, though – that wasn't in the vows.' Gran harrumphed hammily and went to make a cup of tea. Grandad looked over at me guiltily.

'If I give you the money, son, will you go and get some more sausages?'

T-Minus 5 Weeks

"When the odds are hopeless, when all seems to be lost, then is the time to be calm, to make a show of authority – at least of indifference."
Ian Fleming

For as long as I can remember, I wanted to be a husband.

I was five weeks away from getting married and I hadn't spoken to the bride in two days. I know it's supposed to be bad luck to talk the night before the wedding, but there's nothing in lore about ceasing communication five weeks in advance.

Betty had tried phoning me repeatedly, but I diverted all her calls. Not only that, I changed my answer-phone message to a surlier version. Instead of hearing me cheerily invite her to 'please beak after the speep', she was now asked to 'not bother leaving a message 'cos I'll just press '3' and delete it without remorse' (I would later discover that I lost a couple of gig offers that way – one in Kent).

After twenty-four hours of blocked calls, Betty got the bus over to Sale and banged on the door. I hid in the shower and didn't answer.

I was also five weeks away from the deadline for my 39-Step County Challenge. In the first five weeks, I'd done fifteen gigs. To succeed, I would need to do twenty-four in the next five. That would mean hammering five gigs most weeks. I didn't have five gigs most weeks. I did however have GCSE Maths, which made that last bit a piece of piss to calculate.

I arranged to meet up with Tony Vino for crisis talks. We always did something called Kebab Tuesday (which is as self-explanatory as it suggests) so we were due to hook up anyway, but Tony knew something was wrong as soon as he saw me.

'Kindy, Kindy, Kindy - what's up, man? You frickin' love Kebab Tuesday - even more than you love Milkshake Monday.'

'I'm ruining it all, Vino. All of it - getting an agent, getting married. Basically, if something involves me 'getting' something, I will decimate it.'

'Should I get the kebabs?'

'Yes, I'll drop them or be sick on them or something.'

We sat in Al Qud's on Manchester's Curry Mile, and I unpacked why woe was me and everything was terrible. Vino listened intently, fanning his mouth occasionally whenever a bit of chilli seed caught his tongue.

'Listen, man,' he said, once I'd poured out my frustration and we'd ordered two extra cartons of milk to ease the burn, '...this whole 39 Steps thing was always speculative, right from the start. I know you want an agent, and I know that not getting one might mean you never end up closing The Comedy Store or going on *Live at the Apollo*. I get that, Kindy - but is that really what you want?'

I shrugged and bit into an onion. Tony had always been good at challenging me on stuff. In 2008, he curtailed my hobby of ringing up primary schools on a Monday morning and telling them that fictional children wouldn't be in today.

Vino forged ahead.

'You don't have to be on TV to do this job successfully, mate - look at Ian Cognito or Kitson. You love comedy - I've been with you from the start and you've always loved it. And you've always done it 'cos you wanted to, not because you were trying to chase the dollar.'

'The what? Vino, we're not on Wall Street.' #comedyasadefence101

'Yeah whatever, bro. Look, what was it you said? "People don't go into comedy because it makes sense – they go into comedy because it fills their senses."'

'I did say that, yes,' I affirmed, through the oddly resilient onion.

'But that isn't how you're acting at the moment, Kindy. Comedy used to be a labour of love for you. At the moment...at the moment it's just labour. If that's the cost of getting an agent, then, I don't know, maybe the cost is too high? You do the math.'

'...s. You do the math...s,' I rebuked. I had A-Level English, which made spotting that corruption a piece of piss.

'Tony, I'm just trying to provide for Betty.'

'Oh, you mean the woman you haven't spoken to in three days?'

'......'

'And anyway, you're not trying to provide for anyone. You've gone rogue.'

'Is that what people are calling me on the circuit – Rogue? That would be cool.'

'No. To be honest, you're the guy who's starting to annoy everyone.'

'Oh, I see...I could be an annoying rogue, though – like Wolverine...or Rogue. Do you think you could start to spread that as a nickname?'

'Look...' Vino's voice remained perfectly pastoral, '...maybe you should just swallow your pride and sack off the challenge? There's no shame in that, and you will still be a jobbing comedian if you jack it in.'

More shrugging, more onion.

Then Tony smiled conspiratorially. 'But mate, the game isn't up yet. To be fair, this Carlos guy sounds like a complete tool...'

'He is.' I'd taken the onion to school by now and was feeling like a champion.

'Right...so if it were me, I'd give it everything I'd got for one more week, enjoy it, do it without pressure, and see what happens.'

'Can you get me some more milk, please? My face is melting.'
'Roger, Wilco.'
(NB. I can't guarantee that my face was technically melting. I failed GCSE Biology.)

**

A curious thing occurs when you loosen your grip on something.
A football team that has been terrible all season will often start winning games once they're relegated. Nights out have a habit of turning out splendidly when you write them off. The universe, I think, is wired in a certain way so that removing your identity from something, no longer making it an idol, can dramatically change how it plays out. #lifecoaching101

```
Dear Carlos,

Thanks for the picture of  the Cheshire
Cat and the .wav file of some tumbleweed
you sent yesterday — it made me lol and
rofl simultaneously.

Just a quick note to say that I won't be
contin...
```

This was as far as I'd got with my email to Carlos. I was about to jack it in. I had three gigs in for T-Minus 5 weeks, which would leave me so far off the pace that my Sherpa would need to be publicly executed. And anyway, Vino was right: I'd still be a comedian without Carlos. Not a very well-known or wealthy comedian – not one of those comedians who people like or have heard of – but a comedian nonetheless.

But then another email arrived.

It doesn't matter what email I'm writing, if the icon on my Gmail account switches from Inbox (0) to Inbox (1), I have to read it immediately (I'm so excited by this potentiality, in fact, that I've just stopped writing and gone to check my Gmail. Latest score: Inbox (0).)

Saving as draft the email to the agent I would never have, I reverted to my Inbox and found a missive from Spiky Mike, maestro of Funhouse Comedy. The title read:

'Urgent: last minute drop-outs need filling'.

I opened the email and found a list of three gigs on offer. The first one was in Lincoln, which is where I'd been mistaken for a clown and lynched by children - no use. But then the next two were in Leicestershire and Nottinghamshire respectively. To adopt a Panini Sticker analogy, these were 'needs'.

Blanket emails like this get sent out a lot. Spiky Mike had probably fired this bulletin out to a hundred acts. I would need to phone, and now.

'What are you doing, you fool?' I exclaimed to myself. 'You're not doing this flipping challenge any more.'

I dialled the number.

'You can have one of them, Andy. It wouldn't be fair to give you both,' Spiky Mike acknowledged.

'How about I do both, and if I ever turn this into a book, I give Funhouse Comedy an inordinate and incongruous plug?'

When I rang off, I plunged my hand into the waste-paper bin at the side of my desk, pulling out the shreds of paper that had once been a campaign planner and before that had been a Euro 96 wall chart, and started sellotaping them back together. I may also have been cackling slightly, but I can't be expected to remember everything.

I now had five gigs this week! For the first time since this County Challenge began, I would exceed my quota. Yes, OK, I'd still be three behind schedule, but this felt like I was finally taking back some ground and my Sherpa would be spared.

I'd give it one more week, I'd try to enjoy it, and if it still didn't work out…well, at least I'd finished on a high (At this point, I do recall cackling momentarily).

I dissected Notts and Leics with my fat nib, shouted 'Got!' and went back to my drafted email.

> Dear Carlos,
>
> Thanks for the picture of the Cheshire Cat and the .wav file of some tumbleweed you sent yesterday — it made me lol and rofl simultaneously.
>
> Just a quick note to say that I won't be continuing to fall short on my weekly quota. This week is another day.
>
> He who dares wins.
>
> Best regards,
>
> Andy Kind (survivor)

I was back on the campaign trail. I'd been moments away from radioing for a medevac, but Funhouse Comedy had saved the day.

That's Funhouse Comedy. www.funhousecomedy.co.uk

**

I was going back to my roots: to Warwick University (I may or may not have zipped up my boots, depending on whether Odyssey want to charge me for use of their lyrics).
I mounted my untrusty steed, Florence the ailing Fiesta, and rode out once more.

I rang Betty from the M6 to tell her the good news about the 39 Steps. I didn't have hands-free, but I decided she was worth the risk.

'I'm going to take it a week at a time, my lovely. If it gets in the way again, I'll stop…I should be putting you first and I haven't been. I'm sorry, Betts.'

'You're a stupid idiot,' she said. 'And I know you were hiding in the shower. But I forgive you.'

'Coolio!* And it doesn't matter where I am in the country - I'll drive straight back and come and see you. And I'm going to get my wedding suit tomorrow. And I'll buy you some flowers or, if they don't have any, another camping chair. It'll be fine.'

I could hear Betty smiling reluctantly.

'Look, you fool,' she began, her voice brightening, 'Thanks for saying sorry. I'm sorry too. I over-reacted. I don't really want you to stop doing comedy – you know that, don't you? All I want is for you to prioritise hubby-wifey time. You're my favourite person and I want to see you - I don't want to turn up at the wedding and need help working out who the groom is.'

'I'll be the one in the waistcoat that clashes with the bridesmaids' dresses.'

We both chuckled, and then I drove past a police car and abruptly hung up.

I spent four years of my life and fifty per cent of my total life-earnings at Warwick University. I'd been something of a stranger in recent years, and so I thought I'd rock up early and have a stomp around the old hunting ground. This wasn't as much fun as I had predicted, and was mainly a list of sites where I'd been violently sick - a bin, a bush, one of the chancellor's buildings, another bush. At one significant location, I was convinced I could still see the vomit stains, like Thomas à Becket's blood in Canterbury Cathedral.

---

*   Is this quoting? Do I need to get Coolio's permission? I'm so confused.

The curious thing about returning to your past, even after such a sustained absence, is that your mind is primed to adopt an 'inference to the best explanation' policy with the people it registers (I feel now like I would dominate GCSE Biology). So, despite all of my uni friends having left almost a decade before, I kept seeing them around campus - or rather, I saw people who looked a teensy bit like them, and my mind drew a line of best fit. The urge to shout, 'Yo, dude!' as I jogged over to traumatised students I'd never met was almost irresistible.

I wasted so much time and so many friendships at Warwick that, as I ambled aimfully through my old haunts, a desire to go back and rewrite it started panging at my innards. It's not even that most of the misdemeanours hadn't been reconciled, redeemed and forgotten. It was more the wish that I hadn't been quite such a nipple at the time.

Plus, if I'd known at nineteen that comedy was a viable career, then maybe I *would* be on *Live at the Apollo* by now. I'd almost certainly have an agent. The key to comedy writing is the rewriting. It's a shame that you don't have the luxury of that in real life.

But the trouble with nostalgia is that it isn't fully present, and you can't plough a straight furrow while looking back (Or so I'm told – I have very little farming experience).

Still, I was back now, and one last hurrah with a pre-recession hairline and a pre-inflation waistline wouldn't go amiss.

The reminder that I hadn't stumbled through a portal to the early noughties came as I made my way to the Students' Union for the gig. A couple of eccentric, bibbed students (who would almost certainly go on to become out-of-work actors) were flouncing around the piazza, handing out flyers for that evening's R'n'B Night. Every person who passed on their way back from lectures was handed a laminated bit of paper. Except me.

'We don't get many lecturers coming along,' one of them sneered, after I'd forced a flyer out of his grip. I pretended I wasn't offended and got chatting, finding out his name and where he went to school. If I ever did find a way of going back in time, second priority would be tracking down this lad at age six and telling him that Santa wasn't real and he was adopted.

'Cheers, Matt Hardy from Crewe. See you twelve years ago.'

The gig was thunderously good (It feels like decades since I last told you that). University gigs can be a nightmare if the students are in the wrong collective mood, but the majority of the time they're so uninflected by world-weary cynicism that they lap the comedy up. Also on the bill were Justin Moorhouse and Wes Zaharuk - both lovely comedians with bags of jokes (literally, in Wes' case).

Tony's Curry Mile pep-talk had acted like a psychological suppository and I bounded on stage that night like the 'after' guy on an Immodium advert, totally unfettered by pressure. I'd left Warwick an aimless graduate with pipe-dreams of doing comedy. I returned as a professional, smashing the gig to smithereens with exocet precision.

Shortly after draining the pre-journey-back bladder, a group of the academics came to the ~~Green Room~~ corner of the basement where we were standing, and invited us to the R'n'B Night. Wes and Justin graciously declined, avowing that they were too old and wanted to go home. I really should have done, too. But then the last remnant of student in my psyche roused himself from where he'd been comatose beneath some coats, and said we'd be delighted. One last hurrah, eh?

The last time I went to an 'R'n'B' Night, it was still socially acceptable to have memorised by heart all the words to *Miami* by Will Smith (So yes, never). I was still into 'R', and to a lesser extent 'B', but I wasn't really familiar with the Giddy Rascals and the Tiny Tantrums of this world, and so I felt a little bit out of my depth as we entered the mix. The DJ was playing what I presume you'd call contemporary rap music, but what sounded uncannily like swearwords over noise. I hip-hopped over to the DJ booth and requested *Miami* by Will Smith. The DJ gave me a look that said, quite callously: I am not Legend.

Still, I got my drink on (one measure of Coke, one measure of Diet Coke) and I started to get jiggy with it on the dance floor.

After a while, what can only be described as 'a circle of dance' formed – started, as it happens, by Matt Hardy from Crewe and his co-flyerer. Essentially, it's like ring-a-ring-a-roses but, instead of all falling down simultaneously (something, I confess, I thought we were about to do), one by one people leap into the centre of the circle and start freestyling.

Now, when I was eighteen, socially acceptable and didn't look like Plan B's uncle, I remember being relatively good at dancing. What nobody tells you, however, is that at some point in your late twenties you lose the ability to dance like a normal. I'm not joking about this - it happens. In fact, if your age is floating around the twenty-eight/twenty-nine mark, I would suggest putting this book down now and driving around until you've found a local discotheque. Make the most of it – you may only have days left.

It's all about personal evolution, you see. I didn't need to dance anymore. For me, dancing was no longer a means of attracting the opposite sex, but more something reserved for when they recommissioned *Downton Abbey*.

And so there I was, wedged into this circle of dance - and clicking - while the students around me body-popped and shape-shifted their way through the freestyling.

'I must crush you,' I said softly in a Russian accent.

Finally, the moment came for me to trace some serious shapes. Corporately, the circle of dance started chanting, 'Andy, Andy,

Andy'. Rampant with adrenaline, I jumped into the middle of the circle, waited for a beat and then, without really wanting or expecting to...I started doing the twist.

The whole circle stopped clapping and just stared at me. I couldn't hear anything over the loud songtalking and so, gazing around at their befuddled faces, I concluded I had just blown their minds. Exhilarated, and oblivious to the abuse being hurled over the grimy bass, I took it up a notch...and moved seamlessly into the mashed potato.

At this point, the circle of dance disbanded, leaving me in the middle of the dance floor to trace the shape of a bald anachronism. It became clear that I'd outstayed my welcome - by about ten years. It wasn't that the club couldn't handle me, but more that it wouldn't want to without the use of industrial strength disinfectant.

As I was downing the dregs of my Coke medley, thinking about heading back north - back to the future - a girl I'd noticed at the gig sidled over and said she thought I was 'funny and cool'.

'Cool? Were you here for the dance-off?'

'What dance off?'

'Ah, that will explain it.'

'So,' she said coyly, 'you got somewhere to stay on campus?'

I smiled and put my drink down. One last hurrah?

'Sounds fun...but sorry, that's not how I roll.'

I walked straight out of the venue and didn't look back.

Unlocking Florence the outdated Fiesta, a voice from across the floodlit car park shouted, 'Yo, dude!'

I turned to see a bloke I didn't know jogging towards me.

'Hey man...' he said chummily then, as he got closer, his expression shifted and he looked regretful. 'Oh, sorry, mate,' he said apologetically. 'I thought I recognised you for a moment, but you're someone else.'

I laughed involuntarily.
'I know, mate.'

I got back to Manchester at 2:00am, drove straight to Betty's house, gave her a massive kiss and then forced her to take part in a dance-off.
I lost. Coolio.[*]

**

The next few days were sublime. I no longer felt like I was hod-carrying comedy, but had downed tools and was free to enjoy it as nature intended.

Comedy, like any art form, becomes suffocated when you try and regulate it. The moment you start seeing it more as work than art, you lose some of the essence.
That's not to say that all comedy is art. It isn't, I don't think. Consider this: there are only two people groups who have raging tantrums in public - toddlers and stand-up comedians. Sometimes the only difference is that, when we poo our pants in Tesco, we don't announce it.
So not all comedy routines are works of art (lots of them are more like stick drawings with grossly disproportionate peni), but comedy certainly has a room in the Arts' ancestral family home - heckling her cousin Performance Poetry over dinner for being horrendous and letting the family down.

I couldn't go back in time in a physical, temporal or literal sense, but I *could* return to the mind-set I had when I started out on the road less travelled, by seeing comedy as a hobby rather than a job. My only other hobby was sitting at the end of hospital beds dressed as Jesus, so a bit of variety would be wholesome.
Suddenly I was back to my best on stage. I tore it up in

---

[*]   Look mate, you did like one good song – see you in court!

Nottingham; I ripped Huntingdon a new 'A'; I said funny things repeatedly and got corresponding laughs in Northampton.

I even used a call-back – where one of your punchlines refers to something you've already mentioned in your set.

The Leicester gig was another opportunity for Victor Smithers to return to his default factory setting and spread social awkwardness. It was a family show in a marquee, and Victor had been asked to keep it strictly pre-watershed.

'Totes fine!' he had quipped.

He started his set in front of the mixed crowd with the following words:

'How do you take a very small penis and make it ten times bigger? It's not a gag - can anyone help me with that at all?'

When a man in the front row groaned and took umbrage, Victor called him a paedophile.

In artistic terms, it was a comedy stick drawing with an embarrassingly disproportionate penis. Victor was hauled off stage and a performance poet was drafted in to fill time. She ripped it.

**

I woke up in Leicester, thus ticking off another item on my list of 'A gazillion things to do before I die'.

Tony and I had stayed over at a friend's house, and were on our way back to Breast-Shaped Hill* for Falafel Friday when Vino had a mind-spasm.

'Kindy, let's just flipping drive to Rutland and stage a renegade gig!'

'Rutland?! You're crazy, Tony. I like you, but you're crazy.'

'No, seriously, come on – it's the next county. Let's just frickin' do this!'

So we did. We 'frickin' drove across the county line into Rutland

---

* I'm hoping you remember that's the meaning of Manchester?

and bombed around in search of potential audiences that I could entertain for twenty minutes, like the philanthropic joyriders that nobody has ever been.

We stopped outside a pub, went inside, counted the number of tattoos, ran out and got back in the car. We went into a library, tried to cajole some of the silent readers, were ssshed and ejected.

'Is there anything in the rules that says the gig needs to be inside?' Vino asked, vexed.

The rules, in case you've forgotten and can't be bothered to flick back, are thus:

1. You must perform a gig in each of the 39 English Counties within 10 weeks of today's date.
2. Each performance must be no shorter than 20 minutes in length.
3. You must receive payment in excess of £25 for each performance.
4. There must be an audience of at least 20 people (humans only, no animals)
5. Photographic evidence of the gig and venue, and a phone number for the organiser, must be provided.
6. You must wear clothes for each and every performance.
7. If you exceed the period of 10 weeks, for whatever reason, that counts as a fail.
8. If thou dost succeed, thou shalt have no other agent but me.
9. You must never pass my details on to people like Victor Smithers ever again.
10. See the above 9.

'No, there's nothing. But I have no intention of doing a gig outside. Gigs that aren't gigs shouldn't be gigs - remember?'

Tony's eyes were fixed on something across the road. I followed his eye-line.

'No, Tony, no. Certainly not.'

Tony was smiling at a bus depot. Probably for the first time ever.

'I'm not doing a gig at a bus stop. You can get lost!'

'Kindy, we *are* lost. We're in Rutland, which nobody has ever heard of, nor will ever hear of - a place whose geography I have no idea about despite being there now.'

'I'm not doing a gig at a bus stop.' I went on to repeat this sentence twice, slightly faster each time.

Tony stopped smiling at the bus depot and started smiling at me.

'Not even for a Dairy Lea slice?'

You may be too young to remember, but in the late 1980s there was an advert on the telebox containing this slogan. The idea was that kids would do anything for a Dairy Lea slice, which was blatantly untrue, a bit creepy, and generated a raft of Michael Jackson jokes that were still kicking about well into the early noughties, having massively outstayed their welcome.

I won't, nor have I ever been willing to do anything for a Dairy Lea slice. However, as a comedian, I will do most things if, instead of soft cheese, you offer me £100 hard cash. The prospect of seeing his best mate humiliate himself comedically was too good an opportunity for Vino to pass up, and so he opened his wallet and poured on to my lap the lion's share of his fee from the previous night's gig (Tony would tell me later that he would have happily gone up to £250).

'Flippin' eck - come on then,' I capitulated.

'Haha, yes, Kindyyyyyy!'

Tony, giddier than a kid on Christmas morning, strode ahead of me into the bus shelter. We counted just shy of thirty people, who weren't just shy, but totally dismissive of Tony's question as to whether they were 'up for a bit of comedy'. In fairness, it was only 10.30am. People ignored him and carried on talking.

Tony wasn't fazed by this (After all, he's compered Jongleurs).

'Would you please welcome to the stage/bus stop, your first and last act: Andy Kind!!!!'

This was the second worst intro I've ever witnessed. The first was at an open-mic night in Newcastle, where the compere introduced the only black comedian on the bill by saying, 'If you like *The Wire,* you'll love this guy'.

'Kindy, I'll be back in a bit. Have a good'un!'

Tony raced off, leaving me staring down a group of people whose faces displayed various gradations of aggressive inquisitiveness. *Better start with some banter.*

'So...where are you from?'

'Rutland.'

It wasn't going well.

I panicked and went dumb. It was like being an open spot again. This wasn't a friendly 'speaker on a chair' gig, and so I couldn't pass this off as an experimental routine on awkward silences.

'Tell us a joke then!'

Of course, a joke! I should tell a joke...but I couldn't remember any jokes. Seven years on the circuit and I couldn't remember any bloody jokes. Except one.

'How do you take a very small penis and make it ten times bigger? It's not a gag - can anyone help me with that at all?'

'Bit rude.'

'That's not the sort of thing you should be asking people.'

'I might know a guy,' said a man in a trench coat.

I needed to do another joke.

'Erm...my Dad has started dressing as a clown for children's birthday parties. It would be more acceptable if anyone had asked him to.'

'Poor bloke.'

'Is this guy having a breakdown?'

'I wish my bus wasn't late.'

If this had been in a proper comedy club, by now I would have been dragged off stage, thrown out the fire exit and left by the bins.

There are comedians who make an art of confusing the audience with a kind of anti-comedy. Paul Foot would be - and indeed is - my favourite example of this style. He can spend twenty minutes on the decline of shire horses, or write an entire show around the idea of taking revenge on a Bed and Breakfast landlady. Where he is hilarious, however, I am a cretin. I never intend to confuse an audience - even when the audience is just waiting to go home after a bit of shopping. But I was here now and I did need to do a gig in Rutland.

'Look everyone...I'm sorry. I am a comedian, and I've been set the challenge of doing a gig in every county before I get married in a few weeks. If I do it, I get an agent. If I don't, I'm just a guy who tries to perform at bus stops at 10.30am. It would be really helpful to me if at least twenty of you could listen for the next nineteen minutes, and then...and then contribute £25 for my efforts. How does that sound?'

For the first time in my set that day, I got a huge laugh. One bloke in a suit approached me and handed me a tenner.

'I wish you all the best, mate, but I'm giving you this not to listen. I don't think I could take another nineteen minutes of that.' He smiled sympathetically and went off to catch a taxi.

'Go on then, we'll stay.' It was an old lady who looked like a massive witch. 'We'll stay, won't we, girls?'

Her four friends cheered gamely and settled down to watch.

With a mixture of reluctance and resignation, a handful of other people made themselves at home under the dingy bus shelter with the solitary trainer on its roof.

Moments later, Tony Vino came hurrying back towards us, a scuttling plump man in his wake.

'Kindyyyyy!'

Tony threw a cloth cap at my feet.

'Where and why did you get a cloth cap, Vino?'

'Charity shop and to collect money. You can't take a collection without a cloth cap - says so in the scriptures. Oh, and Kindy, this guy is Bryan, the manager of the depot. He's gonna act as invigilator, confirm with Carlos that you did the gig.'

In fairness, you could have hung a coat on Tony Vino's actions at that point - that's how much he'd nailed it.

'Welcome, Bryan. Thanks, Bryan. Let's get this over with, shall we, everyone?'

And we did. Tony timed me using the stopwatch on his phone as I trudged through twenty painful minutes of contractually obliged material. As soon as the timer clicked over to 20:00:00, Vino shouted, 'The End', several people said, 'Thank God for that,' I stopped mid-sentence and Tony went around flourishing the cloth cap for pennies as only he and Dick Van Dyke could do.

Including the tenner that the businessman had put in earlier, we managed to scrape together £11. Bryan, the amenable manager, however, said it had brightened up his turgid life and threw in the difference. We embraced Bryan, held it longer than the acceptable societal trend, and then gambolled our way back to the car, bursting with the adrenaline that the day had engendered.

As a gig in its own right, it had been a complete bus-wreck. Like a joke about Michael Jackson and Dairy Lea slices told in 2001, I had massively outstayed my welcome. And gigs that aren't gigs shouldn't be gigs.

But sometimes they need to be.

**

A week after I considered packing it all in, I had turned the County Challenge on its head, powering up six of the 39 Steps with Olympian power and ruthlessness. I was now, against the odds, on twenty-one gigs: only two behind schedule.

I meticulously laid out the weekly email to Carlos, attaching as a treat the famous picture of Winston Churchill giving the 'V for Victory' sign. Two fingers – one for each gig I was behind. Carlos' reply had no words - only a photo of war-torn London during The Blitz.

I was flipping shattered after the half-dozen gigs I'd racked up over seven days. I'd also ordered my wedding suit, bought Betty flowers and lost two dance battles. We even squeezed in Marriage Prep again - falling as it did on my free night - although it became clear that Clive was a galloping racist and we wouldn't be going back.

'You won't let this get out of hand again, though, honey - will you?'

'No, my lovely. We're past that stage.'

'I don't want us to have another row over this.'

'Look, Betts, it'll be fine. We are past that stage.'

'Did Clive really call them…'

'…He did. Let us never speak of this again. Frankly, I'm glad he got SARS.'

For the first time in ages, my work/life balance wasn't tipping the scales. I wasn't quite 'on course', but at least I could see the track again and, as we headed into the last few furlongs of this grand, national tour, I had one clear goal good-to-firmly in my mind: never to use horse racing analogies ever, ever again.

And all thanks to Funhouse Comedy. Check it out at www.funhousecomedy.co.uk

**

I was back from University for Christmas. I'd just broken up with my girlfriend Jess, and had brought my new squeeze Fran to meet Gran and Grandad.

The velour settee had gone under the knife at the upholsterers, and so Gran had moved some dining chairs into the lounge. We sat on them like squatters, while Fran helped Gran prepare a sausage casserole.

'So, Grandad, what do you think of Fran? I met her at and R'n'B Night.'

'A what?'

'R'n'B, Grandad. It's my favourite type of music. Anyway – what do you think of Fran?'

'Too simpering.'

'Eh? Come on, Grandad, you've got to stop being critical of the girls I bring home.'

'Then don't ask my opinion, son.'

Grandad himself was soon to go under the knife, and his skin had taken on a weird mustardy hue. It had done nothing to appease his sense of righteousness.

'I'm not trying to hurt your feelings, my boy, but I'm just calling a spade a spade.'

'Couldn't you call it a diggy thing?'

'I would never lie to you, son. No, I'm sorry, and I wish you luck, but I think you'll find she's far too simpering.'

'You boys having fun?' Fran simpered from the doorway.

'...Amazing,' I pfffed.

T-Minus 4 Weeks

"The past is never where you think you left it."
Katherine Anne Porter

The wedding was only a month away, and the number of guests was back down to our desired total. In fact, *too many* invitees had pulled out and we were now, somewhat heartbreakingly, fighting to stem an exodus. We were the Pharaoh Rameses of the wedding world.

One couple, recently married themselves, had pulled out because the bloke had got a new job in Iceland and they couldn't make the commute. I have since learned that it was *Iceland* on Solihull High Street, and they just couldn't be arsed. #mumwontbegoingthereagainyouhorriblebastards

The major cause of the shortfall was comedians. I'd tentatively invited twenty of my closest comedy pals in the initial wave. All had said they wouldn't miss it for the world. Most had then pulled out mercenarily as soon as they got offered gigs on that night, drowning my chariot of goodwill in the Red Sea of... erm...comedy.

Victor Smithers hadn't been offered a gig, and was still planning to be there. Dean Gaffney was also still keen.

'Why don't you invite Carlos?' Betty asked.

'Carlos?! But I hate him.'

FutureKind and I were chillaxing at my flat. The sound of *Disney's Greatest Christmas Hits* was blaring out from the stereo. It wasn't anywhere near Christmas, but it was the only CD to hand and we needed something to drown out the sounds of sexual profligacy coming from Pob's room. Sadly, even the magic of Disney couldn't block out the smell.

'You don't hate Carlos, my love,' Betty informed me, 'but, look, you've got to find some way of making peace with him in the event that you do actually pull this off.'

'Sorry, can you not use the phrase 'pull this off' within the current climate? 'Preciate it.'

Annoyingly, Betty was, as usual, shrewder and more attractive than me. Inviting Carlos to the wedding might help pave the way for our future agent/client partnership. I rang Carlos and invited him there and then.

'Ha! Has everyone else pulled out?'

'Not everyone, no...only most.'

'Ha! Well, nevertheless...yes, I'd like to be there. Thank you.'

'Oh...OK...good.'

He must have been having an off-day.

Some of the renegades who couldn't make the wedding had sent cards and presents, and so later that day when Pob had gone out and we'd fumigated the flat, Betty and I sat watching *Ratatouille*, eating ratatouille, and cheekily unwrapping premature gifts. The gifts ranged in price and thoughtfulness, from personally monogrammed dressing gowns and champagne, to four packs of *Iceland* Turkey Burgers.

'Woop woop!' Betty exclaimed as she opened a mangled jiffy bag.

'What is it? A puppy? Is it a puppy?!'

'No, it's a Red Letter Day! I love them...I wonder what it is.'

'Oh, for flip sake!'

I hate presents like this. I have no problem with the concept of a Red Letter Day per se, but I've never been booked for one of these so-called treats that I've actually wanted to do.

As I see it, there appears to be two tiers of 'gift-experience'. First, you have the top-tier, the really good days out: Driving a Ferrari; A Night in a Castle; Dinner in a 5-star Restaurant. The problem is that almost nobody can afford these, and they serve only to make you feel resentful about what you do get. Then you have the bottom-tier experiences, the cheapo days out that I'm always lumbered with: Dry Stonewalling in Matlock; Costa Coffee with John Inverdale; Watching a Horse Drown (with Alf from *Home and Away*). I'd rather have the money.

The Red Letter Day turned out to be a Cheese and Wine Tasting Evening (with Alf from *Home and Away*), and so we decided to keep it. I also kept the Turkey Burgers, for the next time tastebudless orphans came to tea.

My Euro 96 wall-planner had perished like the innards of Alan Partridge's shorts. Having retrieved it from the bin in tatters, I'd worked ferally and a bit tearfully to stick all the pieces back together - but it was no good. Like the Czech Republic in the competition it promoted, the noble planner had lasted longer than expected. But it had gone, its place taken by a gargantuan poster of The Backstreet Boys that my sister used to have on her wall and wasn't mine in any way. #hahasuckers

The great news was that I now had more counties ticked off than not, and all of a sudden my incessant gig-chasing was starting to pay off. Promoters were folding under pressure and booking me for shows in untapped counties. Friends I'd emailed six weeks ago were getting their act together and organising one-off events. Bus depots all over the country were ringing up and asking my price. OK, I made that last one up.

It all meant this: of the original thirty-nine counties on my list, I had only seven left in which to find gigs. And with Tony Vino there to drag me into gigs that weren't gigs, anything was possible (Except time travel, sadly. You've won this round, Matt Hardy from Crewe).

The first show of T-Minus 4 was a hoisting by my own petard, or 'a Clean Comedy gig' as most people called it. Let me explain...

When I was a new comedian, trying to make some headway amid the mass of jostling open-spots, older hands like Adam Bloom and Junior Simpson would regularly say things like, 'Find your unique selling point'. A lot of 'newbs' tend to have four consecutive gigs of awesomeness when they first start. This soon gives way to excruciating pwnage, and makes you realise that becoming a star isn't going to be as simple as you predicted when you watched that *Bradley Walsh Live* DVD. You need an angle, an 'in', and back then it was obvious what made me stand out from the crowd of fellow newbies: I was clean - I didn't swear or mention masturbating paedophiles in every other sentence.

So I made 'clean' my USP. It got me some biggigs, too – both on the comedy circuit and in places where comedy was more speculative.

As word spread, I started being invited to appear on television and radio, to talk about this 'new wave of clean comedy hitting the UK scene'. Tony Vino and I took 'The Clean as Possible Comedy Show' to Edinburgh – a show that packed in a hundred people most days and, unlike most Edinburgh shows, made money (The average net loss is apparently £6000). The tag I'd given myself of 'Clean Comedian' was paying off, and the USP I desperately needed when I started out had worked, pocketing me opportunities and moolah that other mirth-makers weren't getting.

But the problem with giving yourself a label is that people start to label you with it. That's when the trouble starts.

I have never been of the opinion that comedy must be clean. I don't think it should be. Something isn't funny because it's clean.

Comedy has to be funny before it has the right to be anything else - and being funny has always been my sole agenda (apart from when I was six and my agenda was being Lion-O). The phrase 'Clean Comedian' was only ever intended as an adjective, not as a proper noun. The fact is that any adjective bolted on to the front of the word 'comedian' is unhelpful, whether 'clean', 'one-liner' or 'my name is Jim Davidson'. These tags mercilessly manacle the acts assigned to them, and the expectation of a night in their company builds up subconsciously. Be honest: if someone told you there was a 'homosexual comedian' on the bill, what would you expect - a searing indictment against the human rights abuses in North Korea? Or a massive bitchfest?

In 2007, when Bernard Manning died, Frank Carson and I debated each other across several national BBC stations about moral limits in comedy. It was fun, but I'd opened up a niche that was now shrinking to fit. You see, it may well be that comedy has ethical boundaries, but audiences don't come to comedy to investigate that. Nobody turns up at Jongleurs or The Frog and Bucket thinking, 'Well I just hope my latent curiosity about moral ontology is sated this evening'. They come to laugh. The only adjective that really counts is 'funny'. The fact that someone's stuff is clean - or crude, or surreal - should be completely incidental. Does anyone call Jerry Seinfeld a 'clean comedian'? No. Is he, technically? Yes. Does anyone call him a Jewish comedian, even? Not really. Is he, technically? I don't know - *Seinfeld* has no nude scenes.

I may never use Words of Mass Destruction on stage (Indeed, I will often beep out my own swear words in day-to-day conversation). I may just hide these WMDs in an underground arsenal for a special occasion that never comes. But I champion my own right to unleash them at any moment - to use the comedy version of 'reasonable force'. As George Carlin said, 'There are no bad words. Bad intentions and bad thoughts, but not words'.

It's not all Bleak House. The upside to being clean with a small 'c' is that I knew how to properly tear the posterior off a clean gig, and Carlos had nobody on his roster who could do that as well as me. Whether he wanted someone like that remained to be seen, but specialising does make you a specialist, no matter how niche the area of expertise.

One person who could never be labelled with the 'clean' prefix was amoral comedian Victor Smithers. By his own admission, Victor's career had stagnated and, as we drove down to Cambridge, he informed Tony and me that he'd started giving Japanese tuition to students, to earn a bit of extra cash.

'...But you don't speak Japanese, Victor.'

'No, but neither do they. And I've seen enough Steven Seagal films to pick up the basics.'

The gig in Cambridge which started the week was one that Tony booked at JFP (Just Funny People), and he had been wary of letting Victor do the gig because, well, Victor is Victor. So on the way down to that great seat of learning, between ravenous bites of pork pie, Tony and I acted as F-Factor judges for Smithers' provisional set.

'So, I'll say start like this: how do you take a small penis and make it ten times bigger? It's not a joke, can anyone help me with that?'

'Right, well, we've hit upon a problem straightaway there, fella,' Tony said cagily.

'I don't see how. I'd normally say c*ck there, but penis isn't a swear word.'

'No, but if your seventh word is penis, you're already shanking your drives into the long stuff.'

'Yeah,' I added, 'and you opened with that line in Leicester, Vic. It got you booted off stage and replaced with poetry. Why would it work here?'

Victor shrugged dismissively and moved on.

'Right, well, after that I'd normally lurch straight into the bit about shagging my girlfriend from behind, but I'm not going to say that here.'

'Good!' (Both of us).

'No, I'm going to say 'making love from behind'.

'Nope.'

'What now?!'

Tony's face was almost luminously anxious. 'Victor, Clean Comedy isn't just about not swearing - it's kind of the spirit you bring to the gig. Think pre-watershed - you wouldn't hear the cast of *Corrie* talking about making love from behind.'

'One of many reasons I don't watch it.'

'What's after that, Vic?' I was trying to play moderator. It was like the panelists from *Never Mind the Buzzcocks* and *Round Britain Quiz* were sharing a Green Room (I shall want 15% if that crossover ever gets commissioned).

'Well, I've written some stuff about my trip to Amsterdam that hasn't got any swear words or any sex in it. I've penned it specifically for tonight.'

'I'm sure it'll be perfect,' I offered encouragingly.

'Thank you, Kindy. As the old Japanese proverb goes: he who raffs rast, raffs rongest.'

'That's not a Japanese proverb, bro - that's an English proverb in a racist voice.'

'...'

The bit on Amsterdam was nothing if not perfect, and it wasn't perfect, unless the Flemish for 'perfect' translates as 'raging deathfest' – which I'd put money on it not doing.

No, Victor's routine on Amsterdam for the Clean as Possible Comedy Show was a seven-minute invective against people who want to criminalise cannabis. During the darkest moment, I hoped he might diffuse it with a few cheeky Anne Frank gags, but no.

The audience didn't so much heckle Smithers as heatedly debate with him. Tony and I stood stage-right, watching the visible race between their brains and expressions to the finish line of utter disgust. It was like one of those Sunday morning ethics shows, but with fewer celebrity guests and more mentions of the word 'penis'. Victor was never going to win against such a large puritanical opposition (Cromwell was buried there, for goodness sake), and he left the stage early, feeling like the audience had made furious love to him from behind whilst swearing. It was fracking horrible.

Tony wouldn't speak to Victor on the journey home, other than to say, 'Don't talk to me' and 'There were children crying'. Smithers would need a *lot* of Dairy Lea to get rebooked for JFP. *Deru kui wa utareru.*

**

The bus stop adventure had given me a new lease of life and threatened to solve the problem of some of the untapped counties. The following day, Tony and I packed a lovely lunch/picnic and drove north to Leeds, to hijack another group of unsuspecting civilians and to carpe the hell out of diem.

Something on which I often ruminate is this: at what point does a packed lunch become a picnic? Is there some objective gauge for this? Is it simply to do with the fact that you eat it outside? It can't be – otherwise a kebab could technically be classed as a picnic, and that would be obtuse and ghastly.
Having cogitated extensively on the matter, it is my opinion – an opinion I respect, and I think we all should – that the clincher is a pork pie. I've never been to a picnic worth attending where there wasn't a pork pie. Nor have I ever eaten a pork pie without feeling like I should ramp the meal up into a picnic. Feel free to disagree – this is not doctrinal to my way of life. But I am definitely right.
Vino and I stopped at a supermarket, to get petrol and add a

Scotch egg into the picnic mix. I don't like Scotch eggs, but I think that, once you've decided you're having a picnic, it's morally offensive not to have a Scotch egg on offer, if only for show.

Since I'd met Nolin back in T-Minus 10, I had begun to put only enough petrol in the tank to correspond with a year in history, in the hope that other petrol station incumbents might wow me in the same way as that great unwashed hero of Cherwell Valley.
'Pump 5? That's £19.39 please.'
'...Which of course was the outbreak of...?'
'Sorry?'
'Never mind.'

'Why don't we just do it here?' I suggested to Vino, offering him a Scotch egg he didn't want. 'After all, bus stations aren't the only template for renegade gigs.'
'Here? What, in the car park by the trolleys?'
'No, Tony. Inside. Come on, I'm blue-skying this bad boy.'
'Impossible, Kindy. You'll be drowned out by the check-outs and the P.A.'
I smirked derisively.
'Not if I *use* the P.A.'
The idea had come to me as I remembered one of the most surreal moments of my life. It was 2004 and I'd been doing a spot of late-night shopping in Stoke, picking up some frozen doner kebabs and, by way of necessity, toilet paper, when the in-store Tannoy bing-bonged and a voice boomed out: 'Staff announcement, staff announcement...Gavin...is gay. I repeat, Gavin is a massive gay...*bing bong.*'
The other shoppers and I stopped in our wonky trolley-tracks and started laughing at the sheer incongruity of it...then moved aside briskly as one member of staff angrily chased another down 'Frozen Meats'.

Several years later, this would be the perfect time for a call-back.

In we went.

'Kindy, have you got a quid for a trolley?'

'You don't need a trolley.'

'I thought I might get a few bits.'

'Move away from the trolley.'

We made for the Customer Services desk and explained our plan to the generic teen at the counter. The only commandmental stumbling block would be the payment. We briefly discussed having Tony pose outside as a bloke collecting for the lifeboats or something, but we concluded that going to jail for fraud was over-stretching the limits somewhat - and plus, we couldn't guarantee that the prison would be in a suitable county to count as a gig.

We asked to speak to the Duty Manager, and the generic teen rang through.

'Hiya, Phil, it's (the generic teen) here at Customer Services. Got a couple of gents here want to talk to you about something...OK, I'll tell them you'll be there in a min...see ya...He's just coming, guys.'

'Thanks (insert name of generic teen),' I said cheerily.

'No worries. I'm sure he'll be up for it - he's an actor, so he loves all that stuff.'

'That's gr...what?'

'Phil's an actor. Or used to be, anyway.'

In the film version of this, I imagine there will be a grating sound-effect at this point - a dissonant violin string or something.

'Oh no! It can't be.'

'What's up, Kindy?' Vino looked perplexed.

At this moment, Phil appeared.

'It's him,' I said, my mouth and eyes all widening to caricaturistic proportions.

'Who?'

'It's him, Tony. It's Failed-Actor-Phil.'

If you've read *Stand Up and Deliver,*[*] you'll know that one of my first ever comedy gigs was in Withington, Manchester, and was hosted by a failing actor who ran such a dreadful comedy night that it ended in bare-knuckle, saloon-style fighting between the comedians and the audience. Some of the acts on the bill jacked comedy in completely after that, while Failed-Compere-Phil vanished before the end of the night and hadn't been seen by anyone on the circuit since. Until now.

'Hello, Phil. Remember me?' I straightened up to my full height.

'Hi...er, yes, I remember. You found me then?'

'...Well, yes, but not intentio...yes, I found you.'

Failed-Actor-Phil seemed to be under the impression that I had tracked him down with vengeance in mind, rather than coincidentally bumping into him. That was a moronic thing to think - but then he was a moron, so it was logically consistent. Either way, I could use his idiocy as an 'in'.

'Yes, I found you - and now I need your help.'

I told Failed-actor-Phil about the 39 Steps. As he stood there looking squeamish, another memory (like the blood on the Withington pub walls) trickled into my brain. I remembered that, in addition to the fight he ducked out of in Manchester, there was also a gig in Crewe where he'd been down to compere and didn't turn up. His absence had kicked off a string of events that led to me not getting paid for the gig, at a time when I really needed it. I had forgotten that bit. Until now.

'I never got the £20 from that gig in Crewe, Phil. I needed that £20. I still do.'

'You need £25 actually,' Tony reminded me.

'It's been a few years. I'm charging interest, at a rate of...another £5.'

Failed-Actor-Phil looked resigned. Again, in the film version, I think it would be quite nice for Phil to look over to the wall and

---

* You're a wonderful person

see a crocheted picture with the words 'Be sure your sins will find you out'. There's no reason why something like that would be displayed publicly in a supermarket franchise, but that's for the Director to sort out - leave me out of it.

'And if I let you do this,' Phil said momentously, 'then you'll leave me alone? You won't come back to Yorkshire?'

'I can't promise you that,' I answered gravely. 'But I can promise that, if I ever do come back, I won't hunt you down...in the way that I absolutely and intentionally have done here.'

Phil nodded his head solemnly. He agreed. He told us in addition that he was working his week's notice, having been fired for gross misconduct, and we could do whatever we wanted.

'Just twenty minutes alone with your public address system will be fine'.

In an odd way, the little cubby hole where the P.A. sat was the perfect remit for this increasingly wayward challenge of mine. The nature of the busy supermarket ensured that, despite the comings and goings of lots of shoppers, there would always be at least twenty people in the store, while the fact that I was screened off meant I couldn't see the inevitable looks of confusion and antipathy on the faces of people doing a big shop. I narrated into the microphone for twenty minutes, reeling off a list of gags, stopping a couple of times to call for a clear-up on Aisle 6, and to announce a 2-for-1 on all poultry. Towards the end, I tried throwing in a few mind-games, saying things like, 'Hey you, yeah you in the blue coat - I know where you live', until Tony told me to stop it. I sent him to go and buy four roast chickens for the price of two. Our picnic was fast becoming a medieval banquet.

'Get me some doner kebabs, too...oh, and toilet roll.'

As I wound up my set and handed the mic back to the generic teen, Failed-Duty-Manager-Phil shuffled over looking angsty.

'Great stuff, mate, great stuff...Look, I don't actually have any cash with me today, so...so could I give you these Nectar vouchers instead?'

'But they don't count!' I admonished. Nowhere in Carlos' Commandments did it say anything about Nectar points, book tokens or loyalty cards.

'I know, I know, I'm sorry,' Failed-Paymaster-Phil flailed. 'Look, I'll tell that Carlos guy whatever you want. Please, it's the best I can do.'

Ten minutes later, I was sitting pensively in the passenger seat of Tony's Séat. I didn't have money. What I did have was a very particular set of Nectar points. Points built up over a long career of supermarket shopping. Points that made me a nightmare for cash-only tills.

I had left Failed-Life-Phil with a clear message. If he rang Carlos and told him the gig was a corporate and he'd paid me in cash, I would not pursue him. But if he didn't...I *would* pursue him, I *would* find him, and I would make him double the Nectar points or something.

This radical smash-and-grab gigging was totally abnormal, but the abnormality was exhilarating. It was like going behind enemy lines, laying comedy explosives, and then heading back after a picnic. I don't wish in any way to equate myself with the finest fighting force in the world, but this was exactly like being in the SAS.

Except, as I say, for the picnic.

**

It was a wet Manchester morning, and Betty and I were going shopping for wedding rings.

I'd grown to love Manchester since moving north from the Midlands. I was still a Stokie at heart and would cancel most things for a game of darts, but Manchester, I had decided, was the only city in the country that, culturally speaking, could look London in the eye and say, 'This is how it's done, fella'. London, of course, would avoid all eye-contact and refuse to make conversation. Pillock.

My love of MCR was an unlikely one, given my lifelong love of Arsenal Football Club and a gag-reflex that kicked in at the word 'United'.

'You'll probably start supporting Man United now you've moved up there,' morons who knew nothing about football would sometimes say. For the record, I hadn't started supporting Manure since moving to Manchester, in the same way that moving to Helmand Province wouldn't see me develop a soft spot for the Taliban. #coyg

I'm not one to give out relationship advice - I haven't really been in enough successful ones to look someone confidently in the eye and say, 'This is how it's done, fella'. But I do know that the way to massacre a relationship is by mentioning the word *Argos* at any time whilst shopping for wedding rings. When searching for 'the ring', the last thing you want is advice from a lad who five minutes ago was lugging a lawnmower from the warehouse.

Betty and I walked arm in arm through the *Arndale Shopping Centre*, scouting out potential jewellers. Betty insisted on not buying anything that was unfairly traded, and I insisted on not buying anything forged in the fires of Mount Doom, so the hunt took the best part of the morning. It was slowed even further by the almost ubiquitous presence of surveyors with clipboards. In my opinion – an opinion I respect and I think we all should - the human race can be split into two distinct categories: good people on the one side, and market researchers on the other. These are the people who line up at exact intervals along the High Street and accost you if you even breathe in their direction.

It used to be that market researchers were easy to avoid. You'd find a little old dear in a bib asking you to help save the children. Fine. It's a good cause and, besides, she was easy to outrun. But nowadays it's just mental. At 9:30am every morning the market researchers winch down from a Chinook and set up exact arcs of fire along the main shopping thoroughfare.

Walking along Manchester's Market Street was less a romantic promenade, and more like the old *Gladiators* game, *Gauntlet*. Betty and I employed as many evasive manoeuvres as we could – pretending to be on the phone, using other shoppers as a shield, nipping into *Ann Summers* when one of them started pursuing us in an Atlasphere.

'Why can't they just leave me alone? Can't they just get a proper job?' I complained.

'What, you mean like yours?' Betty responded.

'....Yes.'

'Can we leave *Ann Summers* now, please?'

'...Yes.'

I'm not one to give career advice, but if I wanted to buy a new kitchen, I'd buy it from someone who could at least afford to stand inside. If you are involved in this business, please find alternative employment - or at least confine this silliness to London. This isn't how it's done, fella.

Reneging on everything I've just ranted, there is a part of me that would quite like to carry out some rogue market research at some point. You know, get bibbed up, borrow a clipboard and then politely ask passers-by for five minutes of their time - only to then pose completely erroneous questions like 'Can I photograph your shopping?' or 'Would you like me to wash you?'

I suggested this to Betty, and she suggested I wait until never.

After patronising all the jewellery outlets in Manchester City Centre, and after being patronised in most of them for wearing hoodies, we eventually found Betty's perfect ring.

Seeing her model it on her finger and make little eek noises sent a pleasant shudder through my body. With my comedic gradgrindery, the wedding had seemed quite ethereal and far-off until now, but having something concrete to look at made it somehow more real.

'Put yours on, then,' she insisted.

I put a hand into my hoody pocket and pulled out a piece of fabric with a ring inside. My Grandad's ring.

'I'm not putting it on until I'm married. It'll mean more that way.'

It hadn't been the easiest ride so far for Betty and me (at times it had been like driving through rush-hour in an Atlasphere), but we were closing in on the big day and everything was starting to fall into place.

'What do you think, FutureHus?' Betty asked, voguing her new ring.

'I think you look absolutely beautiful.'

It was real. Betty was going to be my wife. My actual wife.

Tick the box marked 'Awesome'.

**

I had a jam-packed couple of days ahead of me and, as a result, had prepared some jam sandwiches as part of a meaningful packed lunch - as well as some leftover Scotch eggs that even human cesspit Pob didn't want.

London was calling.

Technically, I had called London, and some people who ran comedy nights there had said that I could come and do their gigs. Surrey and Middlesex were two counties yet to impose themselves on the back of lead singer Brian Littrell's face, and I'd managed to find a couple of gigs straddling the border of both. I had also arranged to go to see Carlos at the Big Fat Comedy Agency and hand him my weekly report in person. He said he didn't need to see me, but if he was going to be my agent - something that no longer looked unfeasible - we were going to have to work together and he was going to have to like me.

Prior to hitting the smoke, I took a train across to Derby (getting raspberry jam all over my jeans as I tried to eat on the journey) for a lunchtime gig in a bookshop. It wasn't a very large bookshop, and so they had to deconstruct the 'Local Interest' aisle to accommodate the audience. There wasn't that much local interest in the midday gig, however, and so the 'Military History' aisle stayed put. The main interest, indeed, was in whether the red marks on my trousers were jam or whether I was bleeding to death. I assured folks that my wounds were merely psychological and the red stains were jam (A phrase, I wager, not to be found in any book on the 'Military History' aisle).

I missed my connecting train down to London, having rampaged through Derby looking for new trousers. I donated the old pair to *Oxfam*, telling the woman that I'd just taken them off because they were covered in jam (A phrase, I wager, not to have been heard in any store anywhere ever).

Victor was also down in London that night, doing a biggig try-out for Jongleurs in Camden – a gig where starting with a joke about extending his willy might be seen as a bit clean-comedyish. We agreed to go for drinks in town after work.

There are so many gigs in London that it's more than possible for pro acts to 'double up' (perform at two separate shows) most nights of the week. And there are tonnes of great nights down in the capital: Downstairs at the King's Head, The Boat Show, The Comedy Store - all ace. But there's also a lot of gigs that shouldn't be gigs because they aren't gigs. I feel I've been very clear on this point.

The first gig of the evening was a total, undiluted joy. Hungry Miller's comedy night was run by some chaps named Rob Thomas and David Jesudason - a couple of newish acts who, nevertheless, had the gumption and nous to draw a crowd and run a show. Joining me on the bill were Ricky Grover and Addy Borgh – both brilliant. I'd first seen Addy at a gig in 2001 when I was still at Warwick. He was so good even then that I left the Students' Union that night feeling depressed that I could never be that good. I'm still not that good, and it is a bit depressing.

I hopscotched through my twenty-minute set, keen and anxious not to turn up late to the second gig. It was beautiful, though, and as I crossed town via a series of tubes, I briefly entertained the wholly unconscionable thought that London might not be so bad.

The second recital of the evening was a gig that, if it had been a dog, would have been shot through the head round the back of a garage and thrown in the Thames for having massive rabies and AIDS. So back to normal for London then.

The entry fee for this 'concert' was a ridiculous £15 a ticket. That would have been acceptable for the Grover/Borgh combo, but this promoter had committed one of the cardinal sins of comedy promoting – by paying one act to headline and then filling the rest of the bill with fledgling open spots. I was being paid £60 to close the show, but there were twenty-seven punters in the venue, which meant that, after paying for advertising, the promoter would take home over £300 profit - £250 more than the supposed star of the show (me).

Trying to review the event would be like trying to review Rwandan genocide. It was a show to persuade the very ionic bonds that link atoms throughout the universe to give up on life. The new acts were what you might call comedically challenged. One of them could barely speak, being totally off his face on booze. Another was so tit-grindingly terrible that I strongly considered approaching him in private and suggesting he disband. My favourite of the newbs was a lad from the Urals, who seemed to think it was an acting audition and performed a six-minute monologue about assisted suicide in imperfect English. He got the most laughs.

**

I met up with Victor after our respective shows, and we both confessed to having a mixed night.

'Let's hit the Old Kent Road and drink cocktails - then start a dance troupe!'

I could be wrong, but I think Victor had already started the revelry.

He was particularly down in the dumps that evening, having felt like he'd done well at Jongleurs, only to be told in no uncertain terms that he wasn't what they were looking for.

'I'm sorry, Vic. You're still making a living from comedy, though.'

'I'm not really - no. I was, but there's so many comics now that the gigs I was doing once every couple of months I'm now doing once a year. I might jack it all in.'

It was the most emotionally open I'd ever seen Victor, and I wondered whether Robert Patrick from *Terminator 2* had found another way of reaching me. But Victor showed no signs of turning his hand into a blade and stabbing me through the temple, so I put it out of my mind and tried to think of a way to cheer him up.

The opportunity came at Elephant and Castle tube station - the most depressing let-down in use of language since someone put the word 'Party' after the words 'British National'.

Victor and I crammed into the lift at Elephant and Castle with twelve other people, two of whom (one boy, one girl, about nineteen years old) were to all intents and purposes eating each other's faces.

I don't mind the sight of a PDA (Public Display of Affection). Indeed, I think it's quite sweet. What I can't stand, however, is the sound - that horrible chomping, slobbering sound of two people only recently upgraded from snogging their own arms. Exacerbatingly, the metallic nature of the lift meant that the noise reverberated in such a way that we were all able to enjoy this act of teenage passion in horrific surround-sound. It fast became clear that twelve of the people in this lift had ticked the box marked 'Hatred' on the 'How do you feel about teenagers kissing in public?' survey.

It was then that I espied an opportunity both to cheer up Victor and to take revenge on the noisy mouthchompers.

I noticed that the girl kisser had two hands (That's science). One hand she had placed erotically on her boyfriend's shoulder; the other hand was loose, behind her back, *out of sight*.

I'm going to be up front and ask you not to judge me too harshly on this. Please bear in mind that I was trying to buoy up my friend. To achieve this, using one of my own hands, I cupped the boy kisser's buttock - firmly, but I would say tenderly.

Bizarrely, he didn't notice. Presumably, his girlfriend possesses massive hands.

I looked over at Victor, and he gave me a kind of faint, boozy half-smile. I needed to crank this up a couple of notches.

So I started kneading.

Kneading the buttock. The lusty lip-smackers remained oblivious, but progressively the other lifteers understood what was happening and a buzz of excitement rose around the compartment.

As you know, gentle reader, I'm a stand-up comedian. I love to be the centre of attention. And here I was: kneading the buttock with one hand, high-fiving people with the other...being offered small gifts.

Presently, Victor's face erupted into a gurning, beaming laugh as all the tension left his body like those flies from John Coffee in *The Green Mile* (What a dextrous analogy that is, Andy). I'd done it! I'd accomplished my mission of gladdening Victor's heart.

Awkwardly, having got carried away with my Samaritan levels of charity, I'd failed to notice that the lift had reached the surface...that the girl kisser had answered a phone call...and that with both hands now visible to her boyfriend (who still had my erroneous hand clamped to his botty) they had now stopped kissing...and were looking directly at me.

Victor, along with the other bystanders, was now gushing uproariously, while I had no idea how to resolve this. The lift doors had opened, but nobody was leaving before the punchline.

I quickly unmolested this lad, rouged in the cheek and stood there feeling awkward.

And you would hope, wouldn't you, that after seven years of doing comedy I would, at the very least, have managed to utter some semblance of quick-wit?

No.

Sat nav brain kicked in and the best I could manage, in front of the delighted onlookers, was to look this lad square in the eye and ask:

'Excuse me - are those trousers corduroy?'

Thanks, London.

**

'You think you're going to do this, don't you?' Carlos enquired with an obvious smirk. We were sitting in his office at The Big Fat Comedy Agency.

'Yes...yes, I do think that,' I smirked back.

I was supping a Tassimo coffee that I'd made myself. In front of Carlos, next to the framed picture of himself, was a hand-written write-up of the last seven days.

I had done another five gigs over the week. There were 13 Steps left to stagger up, but I was now only lagging by one.

'You still have five counties that haven't offered you gigs, though. And performing at bus stations and supermarkets doesn't fool anyone.'

'I'm not trying to fool you, Carlos. I'm just trying to complete your challenge. It was never there as anything more than a fobbing-off anyway, was it?'

Carlos raised a knowing eyebrow.

'If you'd wanted to take me on, you wouldn't have needed me to go through this rigmarole - I've never heard of anyone else being put through the mangle like this. But I'm a man of my word, and I plan to finish what I started. Do you still plan to keep your word and take me on?'

Carlos stroked the deliberate stubble on his chin, then drew his cheeks apart into a crude, under-used smile.

'I'm a man of my word, too, Andy. You're not there yet, but there will be a contract waiting for you the next time you take that seat. Comm.it.ment.'

'Comm.it.ment,' I replied.

Carlos scanned the burgeoning list of completed gigs on his desk: bizarre gigs that I never would have imagined throwing myself into. I could have weighed in with a speech about how no other comedian had ever been this revolutionary - about how I was a pioneer, a cultural dissident, single-handedly redefining the art of comedy. But that would have been pointless. Carlos saw me for the sketchy stick drawing that I was.

But there was something else. He also saw a man without fear - without scruples. A man determined to prove a point. And I think he liked me at that moment.

'Hello, Manchester? Are you receiving? This is London calling. Ici, Londres.'

I was standing on the concourse of Euston Station, pretending to be a spy.

'I thought you were coming back last night, honey. Why are you still in London?'

'Sorry, I forgot to tell you. I met up with Carlos. I can tell he thinks I'm going to do this! Haha – in three weeks time I'll have an agent.'

'In three weeks' time you'll have an agent. Is that the thing you're looking forward to the most?'

'Ye..eh? No, of course not. I've told you, it'll be fine, you don't need to worry about anything - you know I can't wait to be married to you. But this is good, too, isn't it?'

'Come home, please. We've got place-settings to write.'

'On my way. The rogue is mobile. Repeat, the rogue is mobile.'

'You're twenty-eight and not a spy.'

The line went dead.

I picked up my bag, checked around for double agents, and headed north.

**

We sat together in the park. Grandad was fingering his wedding ring and lost in his memories.

Gran's funeral had been full of peace and joy and everyone had said what a lovely service it was.

'Mum says that you're planning on moving into a retirement flat?'

'I think so, son. The old place is too big for me without your Gran.'

'I could always move in? It would be like Men Behaving Badly...'

Grandad managed a smile.

'No, son, my mind is made up - although some help boxing stuff up will be nice. I suppose the velour settee will have to go. Never thought it would outlast...' he tailed off.

I opened my mouth to speak a few times, then shut it when I realised there were no words waiting.

At length, Grandad took off his wedding ring and put in on the bench beside me.

'We wanted you to have this. Your Gran and I discussed it a while ago.'

'But it's yours...'

'And now it's yours - for whenever you find the right young lady. It doesn't fit me anymore anyway. Just flesh and bone.'

'...Thank you, Grandad.'

'Well, it saves you having to fork out, doesn't it? And it was your Gran's bright idea, not mine.'

'Always full of bright ideas...'

'Aye, she was a good'un, your Gran. She drove me up the wall - but she was a good'un.'

T-Minus 3 Weeks

"The best and greatest amongst mankind are
those who do themselves no worldly good.
Every successful man is more or less a selfish
man. The devoted fail..."
Thomas Hardy

Twenty days to go until I got married.

The local pound shop had a great 2-for-1 deal on out-of-date
Advent Calendars, and so I'd bought half a dozen, pinned one
up next to the reversed Backstreet Boys campaign planner, and
was using it as an inverse countdown timer. I could have just
used an actual countdown timer, or an actual calendar, but who
doesn't love being underwhelmed by bitter chocolate in the
shape of a reindeer? Besides, this way it felt like I was playing
Deal or No Deal.

Hereford was the first port of call for T-Minus 3, for another
Front Room Comedy. We were at the business end of the
County Challenge and I still had thirteen gigs to eradicate with
my fat-nibbed pen. I was frantically ringing and Facebooking
and emailing and tweeting and posting Advent Calendars to the
house of anyone who might slot me on to a bill.

Tony Vino never again wanted to be locked in a small toilet with
Victor Smithers and his stubborn stools, so he opted out of this
latest gig. Smithers, in turn, told me that he was leaving comedy
to go and work with Japanese death robots, so I took Dom
Woodward and homosexual comedian Craig Deeley (What do
you think he talks about? See? Unhelpful). For the two of them,

performing a set in suburban domesticity, speaking a little louder when someone put the kettle on, seemed like something otherworldly. But for me (and possibly for you, gentle reader) it was just another gig. They were the Martin Sheen to my Brando: I was aloof about what seemed to them like a monstrous corruption of a career. I sat in the Green Room pantry, dappled in the shadows, waiting to die. #thehorror #thehorror

**

Betty and I were at the flat, entrenched in the old orange velour settee. We'd run out of Hugh Jackman films to watch, and so we'd converted to Fassbender. I cracked open one of the out-of-date Advent Calendars and we celebrated our new mancrush with glutenous Santas.

I had managed to tie in that week's gig in Worthing (Betty's home town) with a couple of days' hiatus on the south coast for us both. Time together was becoming rare and much-needed, and dragging Betty away from wedding stress was much-neededer. She seemed to appreciate the thought because she kept looking over to me, smiling, looking at Michael Fassbender, shrugging, and then looking back at me.

In front of Betty was a 'Final Countdown' sheet for the wedding. In front of me was the Backstreet Boys poster, with words like Essex, Buckinghamshire and Devon as yet unblemished. I was staring at them implacably, loathing the people who lived there for not helping me out.

A flicker on my laptop screen popped my concentrated hate bubble - my Gmail Inbox had switched from [0] to [1]. Compulsively, I opened the email, read it once, then twice, then leapt in the air and shouted, 'Awooga!'
Betty jumped in terror and emitted concertina vowel-sounds.
'What's happened?! Why are you jumping around? Who still

says Awooga?'

'I've equalised! I've equalised!' I shouted, dropping to my knees with fists clenched.

'Equalised what? Will you please tell me what's going on?!'

'I'll tell you what's going on!' I said. I shall also tell you.

I had just received an email offering me a gig. 'Big deal, yawn, don't go there,' you may say, if you're someone who still thinks it's 1998. But this was different, so I will go there. This offer took my weekly gig tally to five (or as we wrote it in '98: 5ive).

It meant I was level! For the first time since I drove to Worcester in T-Minus 10, I was on track to slam-dunk the funk out of this County Challenge.

'This calls for a celebration!' I declared, leaping to my feet with both arms raised.

I don't keep champagne in my house, so I asked Betty to cover her eyes as I shook up a can of Fanta from the fridge, pounding my chest with defiant glee as I did so.

'Hang on, though...when is this gig?'

'Sunday! Ha!' I was running in small, concentric circles doing the aeroplane as I said this.

'But your sister is coming on Sunday. She's bringing her twelve-week scan photos to show us.'

I crash-landed.

'Damn, I forgot about that...*rubbish eureka moment*...well, I'll see them on Facebook.'

'What?'

'Come on, it's the law of the world that a pregnant woman has to make her Facebook profile pic the twelve-week scan.'

'Andrew, this is Jenny's first baby. She's coming up specially.'

'I'll wet the baby's head with a Fanta while I'm in Taunton.'

I did have a point, I think. I have never understood why people make such a fuss about showing off an x-ray of a foetus. I'm sure it's nice for the parents, but the elephant in the room is that, to everyone else, it looks like someone has googlemapped the moon (As a handy hint, I would avoid using the idiom 'elephant in the room' when chatting to a pregnant lady). I'm not saying that the process of growing a life inside you isn't amazing and beautiful and spiritual. All I'm saying is that, at twelve weeks, you're basically just showing people innards. It's like a radiological version of tripe.

'Look, Betts, it'll be fine.'
'Is that your motto now or something?'
'It's on the family crest. But it will be fine. When this baby arrives, I will love him or her or it like it was my own, but I have two priorities at the moment and neither of them is looking at scaled-up pics of my sister's womb.' I said all this atop the kitchen table where I had climbed up and was holding aloft a vase like it was the Champions League – and singing.
If my motto had become 'Look Betts, it'll be fine', Betty's sigil had become the look of patient perplexity that she was now reprising.
'And what if the gig had been for Friday? Would you have cancelled our trip to Brighton?'
'Of course not! I've told you, we're going to have a lovely two days together. I want to see Jen and look at pictures of her insides, really I do, but you and...you are my priority.'
'Can you come down from the table now, please? And stop singing 'There's only one Andy Kind' – it's probably not true.'
It isn't true, actually. One of the Visual Effects guys from *Children of Men* and *Gladiator* is called Andy Kind. I bet he has champagne in his house.

It's amazing how often in life I can feel like a winner, and yet act like a...well, like a man standing on a table holding a vase.

**

England was almost Sexland. Sussex is a contraction of South

Saxons, while England just means 'Land of the Angles'. We can all be relieved, therefore, that the two tribes divvied the naming rights in that way. After all, it would be great for tourism, but you'd never get anything sensible done.

In terms of location, there can be few gigs more salubrious than Matt's Comedy Club. Set in an old converted cinema, The Worthing Dome is situated bang on the sea-front, the stage overlooking the English Channel. It's a superlative gig, but even if you died epically, getting out of the country would be straightforward.

Having parked Florence the derelict Fiesta outside Betty's ancestral home, we spent the afternoon strolling around the seaside town, arm in arm, speaking like Victorian nobility. Comedians are usually nightmares the afternoon before a gig - we want to prepare and get in the zone, so Frivolity becomes something of an unwanted groupie, forced to hang around backstage until after the show. But a bit of decadent strolling with my future wife was the order of the day, and besides, powering up these 39 Steps had ruptured my comedy groin - I needed some physio, and this was it.

Betty hadn't revisited Worthing for several years and, as she delved back into her own nostalgic archives, the anxious, officious Sudetenland-annexing wedding planner was shorn away to reveal a bright, shining sunbeam of a girl. I experienced one of those moments that are so rare and yet so precious within relationships: that experience of seeing with new eyes the person you're with. It felt like we were meeting for the first time. I suddenly felt the need to impress her, to say the right thing, not to ruin it.

It's very easy to feel young in Worthing. Most of the inhabitants there range in age from '*Countdown* fan' to 'Hang on, I think that was the Duke of Wellington!' It was also, I'm so happy to say, one of the major conurbations to be spared from the 2011 riots. This may have had something to do with the average age of the populous, but equally might be down to the fact that, unlike most urban areas in Britain, a huge majority of the local population carry sticks. Rioters would have been faced down with a huge, shimmering, silvery-haired phalanx, the constituents of which all had battlefield experience from at least two World Wars.

Betty and I passed one of those days that, in future years, may rightly be termed salad or halcyon - lovey-doveying our way round the seaside streets, under the wistful gaze of those who saw in us their own halcyon past. I couldn't wait to wear Grandad's wedding ring.

We drank too much tea, browsed second-hand book shops and did a series of massive tinkles. Down one side street, we stumbled across a domestic salvage shop – like a scrapyard, but with High Street rates. It was called 'Expressions' and boldly boasted on the signage: 'We buy and sell anything!' This seemed to be borne out a few seconds later when a man in his fifties exited with an ottoman footstool, an old Amstrad printer and a cat. The cat, however, just followed him down the road a bit, then got bored and marauded back.

Unlike Brighton just down the road, it's impossible to approach anything like rambunctiousness in Worthing. There's nothing controversial, nothing over-zealous, nothing enchanting. Worthing is, in the truest and most positive sense of the word, very ordinary. But it was against this backdrop of ordinariness that my future wife and I, a perfectly ordinary couple, enjoyed a perfectly ordinary day. And each time we passed a retired couple sitting, hands locked, on one of the many benches which grace the sea-front, our own linked hands tightened slightly, and we both thought how wonderful it must be to be perfectly ordinary together for so long.

Even the gig, in comparison with the chaos that I had vacuumed up before, felt entirely ordinary. Surrounded on all sides by malevolent agents, gigs that weren't gigs, and Victor Smithers, I think I'd forgotten that it is possible in my job to turn up to a venue, be funny, and leave without further footnotes. Worthing was a pleasing throw-back to the old formula: I drove to the gig, I did the gig, people laughed somewhat, I drove away from the gig - my lovely lady next to me.

Laughter is so beautiful in the way it dispels tension. That's why we need it. When you laugh, all the crap, all the stress, all the hurt that has burrowed its way into you gets ejected. It simply isn't allowed to stay. Laughter acts like a sort of leaf-blower for the soul.

As someone whose job is to make other people laugh, the ordinariness of Worthing (the contentious normality of it all) allowed me, for once, to have my cake and eat it - to share a slice of the normality pie. For those two hours, stress was booed off stage.

On Day 2 of our two-day mini-break, we set a course east for Brighton, to visit Betty's Chief Bridesmaid, Dot. We continued the topical strolling theme in Brighton, and I said, 'This is nicer than where I live' a lot. I revised this view as soon as we got to the beach and found that my plans for building a sand city would require me to wait through several hundred years of sedimentary rock erosion (It's how I imagine Joni Mitchell felt on discovering plans had been passed for the Paradise parking lot). I mean, Brighton is aesthetically superior to Manchester, but at least we have the dignity to call a rockery 'a rockery' and not pass it off as 'a beach'. And they don't have as many wheelie bins as us. Cretins.

Dot met us at the beach and the two ladies talked wedding,

while your hero made do with erecting a cluster of large stone burial mounds. Sitting looking over the sea, Betty the wedding dictator abdicated in favour of a gentle peacemaker, smiling and giggling with her best friend about the stuff they'd smiled and giggled about since girlhood. It made me happy to see her in such free spirits...and happier still when some small boys came over to help me construct my catacombs.

Dot and her 'boyf' had planned an evening dinner party on their balcony terrace, and so we headed back there at sunset, leaving my stone monuments to baffle archaeologists for centuries to come.

Dot's studio apartment was the sort of place you walk into and instantly say, 'Oooh, very snazzy' – whether you want to or not.

If the flat was nice, though, more was to follow. On their balcony was the biggest, shiniest, bloodyhellest BBQ griddle I had ever seen. The size of a small car, with totally overblown but awesome ergonomic design, it was the Optimus Prime of the food-cooking world. I stood looking at it, feeling in a deep, spiritual way that my life would never be as good again. It's not biologically feasible, but I'm pretty sure that barbecue was my real Dad.

'Sorry, mate, BBQ's not on the menu tonight,' snorted Dot. Instead, our hostess with the leastess had prepared a selection of what she called 'nibbles and canapés', or what I would call 'not enough food'.

'Will this be OK for you, Andy?'

'Absolutely wonderful!' I gushed, simultaneously using my phone to GPS "hot meat Brighton*". I mean, after all, why would I want a steaming platter of charred animal when I can have an olive and some halloumi? This was a genuine catastrophe for someone who uses 'Man versus Food' as a verb, e.g., I'm off to a Steak House - I'm gonna manversusfood it.

---

*   Which created as many problems as it solved.

I took a plate of nibbles and went to sit on the terrace so I could perv at the Char-o-matic some more.

I was distracted from picking at a quail's egg by a buzzing in my pocket. I mistook it initially for massive hunger pains, but it was really a call from comedian Mark Rough.

'Andy, are you down in Sussex? It's just I've had to pull out of a Rotary Club gig tonight and wondered if you wanted it. Have you nailed Bucks?'

No, I hadn't 'nailed' Buckinghamshire yet. This was unbelievable.

That call, this gig, would put me one up. I would be beating Carlos! He'd been a sadistic mockingbird for the last two months, but that mockingbird would now be shot in the street like a rabid dog in some book I read somewhere.

I didn't know how to react. If I'd been seven, it would have been simple: trousers and pants down, willy flapped. I probably couldn't do that here. So I kissed the Barbecue.

But there was a hitch. I would be too knackered to drive to Wycombe, then come and pick up Betty and drive home, and we couldn't afford to put her on a train at such short notice. I would have to drag her away from her friend, her hometown, and the pretentious spectral food.

When I told Betty, she briefly looked at me like I was a steaming griddle of meat. But then she hugged me like George hugged Lennie in *Of Mice and Men*, and went to tell Dot that we wouldn't be able to stay.

'Andy's just been offered some important work. It's not fair of me to stop him doing it.'

What a wonderful, wonderful, wonderful lady woman.*

Dot packed up a goody bag of canapés for our travels. I went to say goodbye to Sizzle-a-tron.

---

* Sorry, my online thesaurus crashed. Just waiting for it to reboot.

1 7 0

Wycombe-bound, I averaged a 'sorry' maybe every twenty-three seconds, although about a hundred of those came in the first minute. Betty, the wonderful lady woman, brushed off my grovelling with remarkable stoicism.

'No point saying sorry, honey. I signed up for this. You're a comedian - you comede. If I'm going to be your wife, I probably just need to get used to having plans scuppered.' She was looking out over the South Downs as she said this – shielding me from those creases of fear around her eyes.

'You're totes amazeballs.'

'I don't know what that means.'

'Neither do I, but I think it's a good thing.'

I carted Betty and myself sluggishly up the A23 (perfectly sound road) to do a gig that was about as life-defining as standing in a village hall with a group of pensioners. If you possess an IQ above 7 you might have a successful stab at why that was.

It was some kind of Rotary Club dinner, and they thought it would be nice to have 'a turn' as entertainment.

'Do you sing as well?' they asked as we arrived. 'Y'know, 'cos we like a bit of variety.'

'Erm...'

'And you're not one of those modern comedians who talk about stuff like badgers, are you? We just want some good old-fashioned jokes that we can all join in with.'

'Erm...'

I had decided to have a bit of a shake-up with my vernacular, and had swapped phrases like 'I don't sing' and 'Yes, I talk about badgers' with 'erm'. It was a strange choice, but I was happy with it and, crucially, I wasn't going to back out of gigs at this late stage. I needed them all, no matter how tangibly woeful they promised to be.

Sir Francis Dashwood's original Hellfire Club met in High Wycombe. If life does indeed flow in cycles, then the attendees of the Rotary Club were the geometrical antitheses to Sir Francis. There was a buffet to start with, although the crowd shared three sets of original teeth between them, so it was predominantly soup.

After a lot of slurping, I was introduced to the stage - as a variety act.

'So expect a few jokes, a song or two, and even some magic,' announced the secretary, whose tie had been dipped in minestrone.

I have the same level of interest in magic as David Cameron does in people without double-barrelled names, but in the recent and ill-fated vocabulary mix up, I switched the phrase 'I don't know the first thing about magic' with 'erm' (You'll also notice that #ididanothersatire).

The first few minutes were fine. I did some jokes and they laughed open-mouthed, revealing remnants of pea and ham between false teeth. But I knew that my bank of jokes was on the verge of bankruptcy.

With the older generation, there is no time for whimsy. They are just not interested. If you even start to mention jam, you better have a bloody good rationing joke up your sleeve or it's boo-sucks to you. Even 'observational comedy' doesn't work, and any talk of 'man drawers' attracts wry nods of agreement rather than laughs. They. Just. Want. Jokes.

Now I'm not a fancy sociologist, so I don't know why this is. I wonder whether, on whimsy, the oldsters have just come to accept reality as it is, and so squirrels wearing hats just seems unrealistic. The key to observational comedy, of course, is to point out stuff that we all know but don't realise we know: it's the big reveal of what has been hidden in plain sight. Maybe, in your dotage, there really isn't anything that you don't know you know - nothing left to observe? I couldn't say, and I don't wish to patronise - I'm just doing some observation without the comedy.

When my joke bank liquidated, I ventured to distract the golden-agers by divulging that I was about to be wed...much to the delight of the assembled mass.

'Oh, that's splendid.'

'Bring her out!'

'Squirrels in hats, did he say?'

As the playful shouts of 'Bring her out' echoed around the room, I beckoned to Betty to come and join me on stage. The oldies who could stand gave us an ovation, and I suitably bowed and unsuitably curtsied.

'Congratulations, both of you!'

'Don't they look sweet together?'

'*Squirrels? Wearing hats?* Is he a bit simple?'

'Haven't I done well?' I enjoined.

'You certainly have,' said an old boy in medals at the back. 'To be honest, though, she could have held out longer.' A massive roar of approval went up...that turned into a communal cackle...and then into a ripple of hacking coughs. Betty gave me a squidged-up smile and left me on my own.

I had managed to string out the engagement story for so long that, with five minutes of my sixty left to elapse, I had survived on a frugal diet of jokes. But if you're going to give pensioners a really good night, you cannot live by jokes alone.

'Well, nearly time for me to go. One last story...'

'Wait a minute, we want a song!'

'Yeah, do a song!'

'But squirrels don't wear hats.'

They wanted a song.

'Erm,' I said, reinforcing it as my new catchphrase. 'What song?' As though I was going to know any.

'*Underneath the Arches*!' cried the old boy at the back.

'Yes!' they all cheered.

I don't know *Underneath the Arches*, I said to myself.

'I don't know *Underneath the Arches*,' I said to the crowd.

'Underneath the arches...' I started singing.

It's true, though. The only bit of *Underneath the Arches* that I know is, well, 'Underneath the arches.' So for the first three seconds I was coasting. After that, I was crashing off the headland.

So I did the only thing that I could think to do in that situation. After the first line (which, to be fair, I completely took to school), I pointed the microphone at the audience of rapturous septuagenarians and said cajolingly, 'Come on, you know this one!'

I spent the next four minutes (including two reprises) swaying from side to side and opening and shutting my mouth in time, in a vain attempt at joining in.

'Where's the magic?' one of them shouted, as the song wound down and I signalled to Betty to start the car.

'The magic,' I said, ready to leave, 'is that in two weeks' time, most of you won't remember I was here.' I meant it light-heartedly and said it with a grin, and after a good sing-along they were in generous spirits so didn't take offence. I was able to leave with head held high, resolved never to mention squirrels in hats or badgers again.

Ironically, on the way home, we hit a badger on a country lane. It was sad and disgusting, but it felt like an appropriate epithet.

The trek home lasted four hours, maybe ten minutes of which was conversation. Betty said she was just tired and smiled affectionately every time I looked over and pulled a funny face.

'Are you sure you're OK? I asked.

'Fine, my love,' she replied, before going back to her window vigil.

In my defence, I had definitely said sorry this time. Over a hundred times.

**

The next day, I went into Manchester and tried to book the wedding cars. I knew the thought must be knocking around somewhere in Betty's mind that this challenge was getting in the way again, so I hoped that sorting this last major thing on her 'Final Countdown' list would reaffirm for her my part in the covenant. I also texted her every half an hour with variations on 'Sorry, I love you' attached to instagrams of small woodland creatures.

As it turns out, wedding cars are really, really expensive. I don't want to talk figures, but our car budget would nearly - nearly - have hired us a Honda Civic for the day - without a driver.

The revised car budget, that is. In truth, I would have been able to afford a classic Porsche, had I not bought a new Char-o-matic Barbecue online the moment I got back to Manchester. I had viewed it as a wedding gift to myself, but it had taken a large meaty bite out of our remaining resources. The money left was for honeymoon spending, and hiring a decent wedding car would mean cutting down a fortnight in the New Forest to a single day watching a horse drown with Alf from *Home and Away*.

One thing that I'd become expert at throughout this County Challenge, though, was resourcefulness. If I could find a way of gigging in Rutland, I could find a flipping wedding car.

I got on the phone to my mate Harry, who owned a harem of VW camper vans. I told him I needed something that looked pretty, and he kindly offered to accessorize one of his 'girls'. It was perhaps the campest conversation I've ever had.

'I can't drive it, though,' reminded Harry. 'I'm Chief Usher'.

'Victor, it's Andy. I need a wedding driver.'

'Frozen hand.'

'Just do it.'

'...All right, but don't expect me to enjoy it.'

Sorted.

I was so close now. I was knocking off gigs like they were nameless henchmen in a Schwarzenegger film.

Creech St. Michael, outside Taunton in Somerset, was the next faceless villain to be taken down. One of my closest friends, Matt Bradley, was a pastor down there and booked me for an evening of curry and comedy. It was the petition that had seen me mount a table with a vase and chant my own name, and Matt was therefore the greatest hero in the world. No time for socialising, though: get in, get laughs, get out.

Devon was next. The shovel-faced man from the first gig in Worcester had been true to his word, staging a night in a little Plymouth theatre. Behind Matt Bradley, Spadeface was the single greatest man alive. Still, no time for sentimentality: in, laughs, out.

The thought of Carlos' smug face being unsmuggered was driving me on. I just needed to grind out results for another couple of weeks. It wasn't about playing fancy, pitty-patty, cavalier football (comedy). It was just about winning matches (gigs).

You remember what happened the first time I went to do a gig in Kent? Tattooed eyes and male strippers might refresh your memory. Then there was the invitation to Orpington that I blocked when I changed my voicemail to a surlier version. Oh, and of course, the gig in Gillingham that was actually Gillingham in Dorset.

Gravesend isn't a name that tolls with the sound of inevitable triumph, either. It wouldn't be though, would it? Not when it's chief bragging right is that Pocahontas died there from tuberculosis.

I'd been asked to bring a support act for what the "promoter" was terming a "community outreach event". Duly, I put a call out on the Chortle comedy forum for interested parties. A young Australian lad, who told me he'd supported John Bishop and won an award, seemed like a suitable choice. Like most Australians, he was now living in South-West London, working in a bar and making everything he said sound like a question.

He has asked to remain nameless here because he doesn't think the following gig will show him in a good light. I won't name him, therefore, and we'll call him Ozzie. I also wish to remain nameless during this story, but if by now you haven't pinpointed me as a total chaos engine, you are either my mother or a thunderingly literate goldfish.

I picked up Ozzie from Uxbridge and we looped round the M25 towards Kent. We passed a sign marked 'Chatham Docks' and my sphincter trumpeted remembrance.

'So how long have you been over here then, Ozzie?'

'Since March this year?' he seemed to ask.

I thought I was asking him – I certainly didn't know the answer.

'Nah, right, definitely since March?'

'Well, it sounds like it's going well for you, anyway. How many gigs have you crammed in?'

'Ah, you know, about ten?'

'Ten? You've done well to support John Bishop, then. Well done.'

'Ah yeah, it was at a mate's gig last week. John came along and tried out some new stuff.'

'But...'

But, I was about to say and did go on to say, that doesn't count as supporting John Bishop.

A lot of new acts do this. They seem to think that being on the same bill as someone famous means that they've 'supported' them. That blatantly isn't the case. Supporting someone involves being asked personally by them or their agent/manager to perform the opening section of a tour show. Not only is it annoying when new acts do this, but it can also land them in hot water if idiots like myself fail to see through the facade and book them for gigs they're not ready for.

'So this award you won, then? What was it?'

'It was for a poem that I wrote back in Melbourne?'

'A poem? A comedy poem?'

'Nah, it was about Gallipoli.'

'Oh flipping heck.' This lad was a flaming galah.

'What's the problem, mate?' Ozzie was non-plussed.

'Look...'

Look, I was about to say and did go on to say, to class yourself as an award-winning comedian, the award you won needs to have been acquired within the comedic arena. This sounds, I'm sure you agree, comprehensively self-evident. I mean, a comedian's standing isn't augmented by the fact he did Duke of Edinburgh. I for one would be a lot more famous if that were the case (despite setting fire to my tent and a close friend in Shropshire). But nobody has ever introduced a comic on to stage by saying, 'Right, we've got an award-winner for you now: when this guy was eight, he successfully swam a width, so expect big things...'

We arrived at the Scarlet Pimpernel pub in good time and decided to order some food - or, as Ozzie would say, food? The pub was nicely humming with people - mainly industrial-looking men, covered in limestone and smelling of evolution. A few of them were playing darts and pool, some were just jostling at the bar, while others were gathered round the flashing gambling machines.

'Is it in here?' Ozzie asked, finally using the correct inflection at the end of his sentence. I warmed to him at that moment.

'No, don't worry, mate - it'll be upstairs. Don't you worry.'

My young Padawan looked relieved and encouraged. It's nice to be in that position, where you can reassure younger comedians with the experience of several hundred gigs. I was Qui-Gon

Jinn.

The organiser emerged from behind a one-armed bandit and came over to present himself.

'Hi, mate. Presuming there's a function room upstairs for the gig?'

'No, it's down here.'

'...I see, and you'll clear the venue in a bit and then they'll have to pay to get back in?'

'Er, no, it's a free gig. People can just turn up as and when. Good numbers, though - most of them are here for the comedy.'

Ozzie, my young Padawan, looked up at me petrified. I was no longer Qui-Gon Jinn. I was Jarjar Binks.

The gig, the truth outed, had an organiser who hadn't organised anything beyond asking permission from the landlord to be there. It was like an upside down comedy pageant - everything you would hope for at a comedy night had been inverted. The stage (carpet) was the only corner of the pub where there wasn't a gambler. The mic would have looked archaic when *Top of the Pops* first aired. The spotlight was the fading, shrivelling light seen before the soul departs the body. Naked mole rats burrow up to two metres deep – none is this badly lit or amplified.

'Have you got wifi here?' I foolishly asked the manager as I ordered a Hunter's Chicken. He looked at me as though I'd geo-cached his kids and handed him the co-ordinates.

Ozzie and I sat at a table, saying little.

'I'm gonna die up there, aren't I?'

'Don't talk like that! You've got to stay positive,' I cooed, before going outside to ring Betty, tell her I loved her one last time and she must never marry.

The promoter acted as the Master of Ceremonies, by turning on the mic, standing next to it and saying, 'Right, we've got some comedy tonight - hope you enjoy it. Over to the first comedian... Australian.'

'Have a good'un, Ozzie.'

Ozzie went up and, to his eternal credit, tried really hard. When the promoter had said that most people were there for the comedy, he was right, but also, he was amazingly wrong. Nobody was there to enjoy the comedy. They hadn't had to pay to get in, they weren't even asked to pay attention and not talk or play *Pétanque*. The landlord had agreed to turn the jukebox down but not off, because, y'know, not everyone wanted to listen to the comedy. Ozzie was initially ignored, but then, as though all these grit-covered tradesmen were piranhas and they'd just noticed a coy carp dropped into their tank, Ozzie got eaten alive. The heckles were merciless…

'Back to the scene of the crime, mate?'

'Sh*t at cricket, sh*t at comedy!'

'I've got a question - when are you leaving?'

'Sshhhh…'

Even the promoter could now see what he'd done, sending that poor young Australian lad to die. *Something about Gallipoli*

'Look, Andy, it's not working is it? I'm sorry. I'll pay you full fee, but you don't need to do the gig.'

'Of course I'm doing the gig!' I bristled.

'Eh?'

'You're right, mate, this is a complete shambles and you should be a little bit ashamed. But I'm not leaving Kent again without doing my twenty minutes. Besides, it's not fair on Ozzie. And besides Part Two, my Grandad was at Arnhem. I'm doing the gig.'

I'd been air-dropped into enough danger zones within the last two months to know that this would be carnage. But it was my job. My Grandad didn't get halfway across the English Channel, bottle it and say, 'Oh, sorry, when you said 'Market Garden', I thought you meant like a National Trust property – shall we head back?'

I'd crossed a bridge too far weeks ago. Grizzled and battle-hardened, I was just totally numb to it now. *Utrinque Paratus.*

I went on and dug in. I gunned down the first few hecklers, but there was always someone else to step into the breach. I wasn't so much outbantered as spoken over. It doesn't matter how many gigs you've done, or what awards you've won (genuine comedy ones that aren't poems) – until you're famous, no audience cares who you are or what you've achieved. You are always starting from scratch and, if a group of guys in a pub wants to sing along to Johnny Cash on the jukebox or have a *Boules* tournament, that's their prerogative.

Towards the end of my set, I was concentrating as much on a conversation at a nearby table as I was on my own material (It was about Holiday Property Bonds and I've since done some research). I got to twenty minutes, by which time only Ozzie and the promoter were still listening, raised my arms in mock triumph, and evacuated.

We left the Frenchly named pub that evening having put the 'come, die' in *comedie*.

Ozzie (shell-shocked, his thousand-yard stare present and correct) spent the journey back to Uxbridge asking more questions that weren't questions. I replied with answers that weren't answers. It's what happens when you do gigs that aren't gigs. Bless him, though - he deserved an award for that. And a medal of honour.

**

Looking back through my diary for the week, Worthing felt like a seaside resort on a coastline otherwise strewn with shipwrecks and oil slicks. Delving back even further - the mass pile-on in Lincoln, the police intervention in Chester, the bus stop, the supermarket, the bookshop, everything about Kent - I apprehended just how unequipped some comedy gigs are for comedy.

Sometimes, you get the impression that 'promoters' are making a conscious effort to crush your spirit, to do the complete opposite of what you ask them. Some gigs are so epically bad, the survivors hold periodic reunions in the style of the Titanic.

Nevertheless, a massive week was over. The wedding list was practically complete. And...

I was one gig ahead of freakin' schedule! I had seven gigs left to do and remarkably only two counties left to tap up - Durham and Essex.

I could see the top of the 39 Steps.

I had no reply from Carlos that week. No snidey retort, no horrific pictures. He had nothing. Shame, because I'd activated my auto-reply function to say, 'Sorry, I'm away from my desk, dancing in my pants and serving up huge portions of win.'

Next week would be packed to the rafters. I had four gigs in the diary, plus my stag do was looming. On all fronts, it was nearly party time.

I didn't tell Betty what sort of wedding car she was having, nor did I mention the wedding gift of the Lovematic BBQ. I would reveal them as surprises nearer the time.

But I wasn't the only one with a surprise up my sleeve.

**

It was Christmas and we were all ensconced within Kind Towers. The paperwork for Grandad's flat at the retirement home hadn't been finalised, and so he was staying with Mum and Dad in the interim.

I had no new girlfriends to flourish, which was a relief. Gran's death had taken the grace out of Grandad's honesty and left it blunt and gratuitous. Nobody really minded, but it would be a blessing not to be told that my choice of girl was 'too flighty' or 'too simpering' - or something worse.

I was upstairs on the computer, playing on Call of Duty 2. *One of the missions required you to play as a trooper in the British 6th Airborne Division, drop into Benouville and take Pegasus Bridge. Grandad had been there in '44 - dropping into Fortress Europe in the following wave, crossing Pegasus Bridge en route to his post.*

'What are you doing, son? What's that noise?' It was Grandad on the landing. His voice was thinner and his body more frail these days, but his interest in his grandson had lost none of its vigour.

'I'm in here, Grandad.'

Grandad hobbled in on his stick and stood transfixed by the bright screen.

'What is it?'

'It's a computer game – you...er...you have to take Pegasus Bridge.'

'Pegasus Bridge, eh?'

Unsure how Grandad would take the transforming of his harrowing past into a video game, I grimaced slightly and studied his expression. Then, on cue, sat nav brain locked on.

'...Would you like to have a go, Grandad?'

Grandad turned his callow face towards me, raising an eyebrow.

'Would I like to have a go? I'm eighty-five years old, son...'

'...'

'...of course I'd like to have a go!'

Grandad rested his stick by the computer chair and sat down at the controls. At that moment, a German soldier appeared on the screen, MP40 machine gun clacking away.

Setting eyes on the Panzergrenadier, my Grandad, the frail former elite paratrooper, raised his hand, pointed at the screen and said:

'Hello there, Fritzy – guess who's back?'

T-Minus 2 Weeks

"Love is not affectionate feeling, but a steady wish for the loved person's ultimate good as far as it can be obtained."
C.S. Lewis

A fortnight to go. With Betty an immovable object of beauty at my side, I was heading with irresistible force towards my dual goals. In fewer than two weeks, Betty and I would freely say 'I do', while Carlos would be contractually obliged to. It was all pleasantly nauseating. My to-do list for the wedding was garnering tick after tick - and would have fared even better if one of the tasks had been 'Experience several daily bouts of vicious diarrhoea'. But that would be cheating.

Emma, the producer of Andy Crane's radio show, rang to book me in for the first Sunday after my honeymoon.
'Presuming that you're still on course to complete it?'
'Yes, u-huh, absolutely, cool, cool, that's...yooooo.' It was classic agreeing-to-something-prematurely-when-the-threat-of-total-failure-was-still-very-real etiquette, and I'd nailed it.

Lancashire, Cornwall, Norfolk, Hampshire, Gloucestershire, Durham and Essex. Seven more *aller-retours* and I'd be done. Like the Eye of Sauron, my will was bent on the last two of that stubborn group, scouring their nooks and crannies for those final two steep, hidden Steps.
I stumbled upon one of the two almost instantly. My friend Marko was a youth worker and had managed to wangle me something in his neck of the woods. So on a Tuesday morning, when I should have been giving my alarm clock the V-sign and

going back to sleep for three hours, Florence the 'not long for this life' Fiesta drove me up to Darlington to do an assembly for three hundred school kids. At 8.50am, they were expecting a gentle philanthropic message, not a bullet-proof club set from a professional comedian. I charged through it, impregnable to any reaction whatsoever. The word to describe it was 'harrowing', but I couldn't have cared less. I left as quickly as possible, thanking Marko and refusing to answer the Headmaster's questions about CRB checks.

'Kindy, what the hell do you mean you're not going to be here for Kebab Tuesday?' Vino berated me.
'I'm off to East Anglia, bro - let's do it tomorrow.'
'On a Wednesday? Kindy, it's not called Kebab Wednesday. It is, and always has been, Kebab Tuesday - that's why we hold it on a Tuesday. I can't believe you're saying this to me - you've finally lost it!'

I drove straight from Darlington to Norwich (a mere five hours) to perform at a meal for some homeless guys. They sat around tables eating pizza and chips, and Robo-comic went through the pre-programmed routine. The word to describe it was 'harrowing', but it was nice for the vagabonds to think that there was someone worse off than them. As a lovely bit of feedback, one of their dogs bit me (Prowled over part way through the set, tilted his head curiously and bit me. Then prowled back to his master, a bit of rope trailing from his collar, and curled up with a pizza crust). I should have known better really. After all, it's one of the first things they teach you at comedy school: don't stare at the floor; don't fiddle with the mic lead; don't get bitten by a dog.

By 10:00pm on that Tuesday evening, I'd driven six hundred miles and spent nearly twelve hours behind the wheel. The long-distance comedy courier delivering jokes. Jokes returned to sender.

It didn't matter. It just didn't matter. Five gigs to go.

Five Steps to climb. One to find.

(By the way, don't forget about Funhouse Comedy. Your one-stop shop for comedy nights in the East Midlands and beyond!)

I was running on a mixture of fumes and auto-pilot, looking forward to marrying the love of my life and having two weeks away from the cuckolding claws of Old Lady Stand-up. But nothing focuses your mind quite as well as four hundred people rammed into a proper comedy club. It was a searingly strong line-up at Jesters in Bristol that Thursday, with Liam Mullone, Geoff Norcott and Alistair Barrie on the bill, and so going at it half-cocked would be a phrase I'd regret using pretty much as soon as I wrote it.

There was a proper Green Room for once, with beer and sandwiches and a sense that you were in some way wanted. I'd missed that recently. I had never insisted on a rider, but I decided that once I got back from honeymoon I would start demanding one at every venue. Two bottle of Leffe Blonde - and a live puma to look at.

Geoff had just got back from a gig in Dubai, while Liam and Al had been flying around the biggigs of Britain, asundering venues left, right and centre, not getting ravaged by Dalmatians. 'You been busy too, Andy?' Geoff enquired as we stood backstage, waiting for the intro music to announce me as compere.

'Yep. Kids and tramps mainly. Probably do Dubai next year. Or a funeral.'

The music rang out. I pulled back the curtain to the stage.

'Have a good'un, mate.'

It felt like aeons since someone who wasn't my own pallid

reflection told me to 'have a good'un.' Normal gigs were needles in a haystack upon a camel's back long since severed by too much straw.

'Hello, Bristol! I'm Andy, I'm your host and guide through the next two hours of cachinnating cacophony.' A woman at the front whooped (Presumably, she had that sentence in the Guess-how-the-compere-will-start-the-show sweepstake). It was already, by some distance, the best gig of the week.

'I live in Manchester, but I'm originally from Stoke-on-Trent.'

'Woo!' Another solitary cheer went up.

'Hang on...are you guys playing bingo with everything I say?'

The lights were so bright that I couldn't really see past the first row of punters, and so trying to gaze into bleary darkness provided me with no clue as to the cheerer's origin.

'Woo, you say? Are you from Stoke, or did you just have it in the Guess-where-the-compere-was-conceived sweepstake?'

'I'm from Stoke.'

'Oh cool. Whereabouts?' I followed up.

'Newcastle.'

'Me, too!'

'I know,' came the flat response.

I told you in T-Minus 6 that I've only once in my career been completely undone by a heckle.

Well, this is it.

Heckles in the shape of words are not something that frighten me. But if there's one thing that is going to leave me paralysed, it's a heckle in the shape of a familiar face.

'How do you know I'm from Newcastle?' I asked the heckler.

There was a hush in the auditorium - which lasted long enough for my mind to put a trace on the voice.

Oh no...

'Because we went out together for four years.'

Shading my eyes from the interrogatory spotlight, I gazed

through the murkiness of the club, scouring the crowd for confirmation. Then suddenly I found it or, rather, found her.

Jess.

And everything I've said about comics being equipped to deal with hecklers became blunt and redundant.

Jess, to recap, was my childhood sweetheart. I'd briefly ruined her life with my horrific infidelity and the last time I'd seen her I'd said sorry for doing that and we both bawled our eyes out on her doorstep because she almost died from cancer but then didn't. Recap accomplished.

But what was she doing here, and why now? I felt settled that the whole relationship had ample closure. I didn't really want to see her again – particularly part way through a stand-up set with several hundred people watching me. And yet here she was, a week before my wedding, looming out of the past to stare into my soul.

Comedy is about recognition. In any classic British sitcom, a lot of the laughter emanates from our relief that the things taking place aren't befalling us. Add to that the fact that we're a nation who slow down for car crashes and cheer at smashed plates, and it's easy to see why the tenterhooked crowd, on being brought up to speed with 'Ladies and gentleman, my ex-girlfriend', erupted in the most callous outburst of laughter I've ever had the misfortune to be the brunt of. People were whooping, snorting, hootenannying: in a nutshell, they were loving it.*

'Well,' I stammered, staring at the floor and fiddling with the mic lead, 'I think the only thing here is to bring on one of the comedians.' I waved Geoff to the stage.

'Does anyone here have a history with Geoff Norcott?...No?...Good, then this will be less awkward than the last minute...'

I went and stood at the back of the venue and waited. For Jess.

---

* For a while there, I didn't think I was going to get chance to use the word hootenanny in this book. Phew.

As I suspected, she sought me out immediately, smiling as she drew nearer. Her hair was blonder now, but her signature dimples were still masterpieces.

'What are you doing here, Jess?' I asked, without accusation.

'I live in Bath, Andy - remember?'

'I know, but this is Bristol.' Sat nav brain was on the blink.

'Oh really, is it?' Jess mocked chummily. 'Listen, I didn't even know you were on - I just fancied a night of comedy. But, hey, I've never seen you gig, so it's about time. It's good to see you, Andy.'

We chatted for the twenty minutes that Geoff ripped up the room. Jess, I learned, was newly married and had twin baby girls. Her dimples creased pronouncedly as she talked about them.

'Are you with someone?' she asked, without bitterness.

'I'm getting married next week, actually.'

'Wow, congratulations!' She held out her hand for me to shake. I laughed at the strained formality of it.

'I'm glad we both found the love of our lives eventually, Andy...'

'...Me too.'

I stopped short of inviting her to the wedding. We had the space (Dean Gaffney had pulled out), but maybe that was one courtesy too many.

During the second half of the show, I looked over to see if Jess was enjoying it. Her seat was empty. She hadn't just 'fancied a night of comedy' at all. I don't really know why she came. But it was good to see her. I love happy endings...

**

The weekend of the stag and hen had finally arrived. The taxi taking me to the station beeped its horn outside the flat. Unable to process such levels of excitement, I had no choice but to pull down my pants and flap my willy.

Pob hadn't been invited to the stag do (I found him more annoying than films where illiterate mutes witness murders). I had decided, furthermore, that the best ploy was to avoid mentioning it in the hope that he wouldn't notice.

'You off somewhere special, Andy?' he asked as I lugged my bag to the waiting taxi.

'No, mate - just off to a gig.'

'But you're dressed as Optimus Prime.'

'No, I'm not.'

Simples.

Betty and her girlies were staying in Manchesterford for the weekend, for a blow-out session of arts and crafts and tea. Me and the lads were hitting Brum, for farts and laughs and WKD. And ritualistic shaving.

We were due to meet at the train station at 6.30pm, already dressed in our outfits. Tony and Harry, superintendents over the weekend, had made the decision that we should all dress as our favourite superheroes. Subsequently, from about 6:00pm onwards, Birmingham New Street station saw a gathering of fiction's greatest icons. Superman got off the 6.03 from Bristol Temple Meads; The Hulk alighted from the 6.07 from Coventry; Big Pappa Smurf arrived from Stoke.

Not everyone had arrived without issue. Victor Smithers had noted that a waistcoat and several necklaces might not keep him warm on his journey by coach, so had vested himself in a long overcoat. Unfortunately, the rest of his Mr. T costume (a blacked-up face) was visible to everyone riding the National Express from Manchester. By the time he joined the ever-burgeoning throng, he had been called a racist six times, a bigot five and 'a legend' by two members of the English Defence League.

By 6.30pm, everyone had turned up and we were ready to hit the town – or, more likely, get hit in the town. Martin, a slightly awkward lad I went to school with, was the last person to check in. By this stage, from a group of fifteen lads, most had dutifully followed the rules and come dressed as obvious heroes of some form. We had a Spiderman, a Batman, two Wonderwomans, a Gladiator and a Captain Planet (I've already told you that I was dressed as Optimus Prime, but then I often dress as Optimus Prime, so it was no biggie). A couple of the boys had obviously felt that hiring the proper costume was too much hassle and so had just rummaged around in their wardrobes for vestiges of previous stag dos and fancy dress parties. Amid the superhuman talismen of goodness, therefore, there was an Umpa-Lumpa, a John Travolta and, perhaps the greatest superhero of them all, Bjorn Borg.

But at least everyone had come in an outfit that made them stick out from every single other person on the station concourse. Imagine our corporate confusion and slight disgust, then, when Martin turned up in a tatty suit and tie, carrying a briefcase.
'Crazy fool!' shouted Mr T.
'Don't make me angry!' added The Hulk.
'You f***ing coward!' exclaimed Big Pappa Smurf, failing to grasp the game.
Martin looked totally crestfallen. Harry (dressed as Jesus) parted the crowd.
'Hang on, gents, calm down. Now Martin, you know this is a superhero stag do. Which superhero have you come as?'
There was a pause as Martin failed to make eye-contact with the Good Shepherd and instead looked sheepishly at his own feet.
'I've come as my Dad,' he finally muttered.
It was a wonderfully sweet thing to say, ruined by the fact that everybody, Jesus included, laughed uproariously in his face.
'Why are you laughing?' Martin challenged, emboldened. 'My Dad has never had a great job, but he's worked really hard all

his life to provide for me and my Mum. I've never wanted for anything. That's what a real superhero is. Laugh if you want to, I don't care. My Dad *is* my hero.' Nobody laughed (By the end of the evening – albeit drunkenly – all of us had rung our Dads, just to say thanks). And for the rest of the night, passers-by observing the group saw a scrawny guy with a suit and briefcase surrounded by fourteen superheroes. Martin looked like a VIP accountant.

'With you I am well pleased,' Harry said, embracing Martin. 'Right, come on, the restaurant's booked for 7:00pm. Follow me.' And then, wading deeper into a blasphemous mire, Harry led the way into the city.

Most of the evening cantered along jauntily, all of us growing comfortable with our anomalous outfits and starting to relax in our surroundings. The waiters in *Shimla Pinks* on Broad Street treated us with a playful reverence, graciously accommodating us in our juvenile stupidity. They laughed politely when Mr. T (Smithers) insisted that he must have a Peshwari Naan because, and I quote, 'I ain't getting no plain, fool.' It was a joke he had been waiting to tell for several hours and he sat there smugly for the next two minutes, basking in his own glory. Shortly afterwards, he approached the same waiter and confided privately that he didn't like coconut, and could he, in fact, have a Plain Naan.

The waiters were more confused when, on enquiring whether we'd like wine with our meals, Harry, by now almost entirely convinced that he was the Messiah, cockily asserted, 'No, just several jugs of water – I'll sort the rest.' Again, one of us had to scurry after the bemused waiter, explain the joke and ask for several bottles of house red.

It's amazing, ironically, how unthreatening a big group of lads seems when dressed as invulnerable icons. I think it's something to do with subverting your own sense of bravado and pretension. Anyhow, it led to a lovely feeling of community, not just within the group, but without. Just before we left the restaurant, having consumed the whole cast of *Chicken Run* in a variety of sauces and guaranteeing that anyone sitting next to us on the return train would be paying £15 for the First Class upgrade, two police vans shot past us along Broad Street. A lady on the table next to us, dining with her young family, leaned over to Spiderman and said, with mock earnestness, 'Shouldn't one of you guys do something?'

On our way to Reflex, where we planned to crank the evening up a notch, I rang Betty to ask how she was getting on.
'Just finished painting some pottery and about to watch *Love Actually*, my love. What are you doing?'
'Same. Love you, bye.'
And so to Reflex, the 80s bar. Not the most 'street' of places, but it's one of the few places hospitable to ne'er-do-wells like ourselves, and besides, we weren't going to get within a hundred metres of an R'n'B club - not with Victor's face-paint (In addition, when you've been to private school and acquired a degree in Modern Languages, it's almost irrevocably taxing to be 'street'. I can just about manage 'country lane').

I had assured Betty that I wasn't going to get hammered, and so I did my best to stick stoically to the one part Coke, one part Diet-Coke cocktail. That plan was ransacked the moment Bjorn Borg ordered a dirty pint 'with all the trimmings' and double-dared me to down it.
'He's just a chicken!' clucked the bitchier of the two Wonderwomen.
The Marty McFly mural told me all I needed to know. I took the pint and downed it (stopping part way through to check if there was an eye doctor on hand because I could feel my retinas melting).

The evening wound down and Harry started to think about dredging the staglings from the gutters and leading us back to the Comfort Day Lodge Travel Inn or something. I was a mess. My liver still hadn't forgiven me for my early twenties, and so getting drunk was akin to saying, 'I'd like to pay £50 to vomit, please.' However you look at that, it's not a good deal. The dirty pint had surged through my body like an unstoppable rebel force and was now staging a coup on my internal organs. My liver was penning a suicide note.

I tried to text Betty to apologise for getting hideously drunk, but I had forgotten where my fingers were and what they did.

What I hadn't noticed was that another stag do, similarly outfitted with the same sartorial elegance, had entered Reflex and was now making its way to the dance floor. Despite being dressed as the leader of the Autobots, I was completely oblivious to any hint of danger.

Suddenly a harsh, jutting finger prodded me in the back. I turned sluggishly, refocused my ever-blurring vision, and then tensed. Standing right in front of me, through the hazy sweatiness of the 80s bar, was Megatron.

(It would be revealed later that his real name was Craig, he was an actuary in his late thirties and he was getting married on the same day as me. But I didn't care for any of that. All I saw was a nemesis).

'A dance-off, Prime,' barked Megatron.

I looked around me. The dance floor had suddenly been laced with giddy punters, delighted by this serendipitous encounter between two intergalactic foes (from the Midlands). Craig's boys were fresh, sober, sparkly in their bespoke costumes. My staglings had been scattered. The ones who hadn't gone to hospital or dozed off in the corner painted a sad picture of desolation. An unmasked Spiderman, suffocating in his spandex; a grotesquely hirsute Wonderwoman flashing his hairy man-boobs; a 1970s tennis player who had lost his racket, wig, moustache and, oddly, his shorts.

The only man among us still in full costume and totally *compos mentis* was Martin. Not leaving the dance floor once all night, save to replenish his bottle of water, he still wore his Dad's old suit and swung his briefcase with pride and gusto. He would have appeared a fine ally in the current conflict, if he had actually dressed like one of us and not simply like a normal bloke.

Craig's boys were mocking us, taunting. I knew what I must do. Megatron must be stopped – no matter the cost.

Brushing past him with my shoulder, I marched onto the dance floor. Then, turning to face him head on, I said the only thing I could possibly say in such a situation.

'One shall stand; one shall fall.'

Crushingly, Craig, not having been spiked by his best mates, was in fact able to stand. I, feeling as though the whole room was spinning down a plughole, couldn't help but fall – flat on my back, smacking my head on the floor as I did so.

All I saw was darkness. Noisy, sickly darkness. Was this death? All of a sudden, I found myself being hoisted to my feet. Head ringing, I opened my eyes and was blinded by the lights from the ceiling. Then, silhouetted against the brightness, helping me back up, I saw him: Jesus.

He'd just come back from the toilet.

**

'Did you have a lovely time, my love?' Betty asked. It was Sunday morning and she was round at our new house, decorating for once we moved in after the honeymoon.

'Boilk,' I managed by way of response. And then, after a few seconds, 'Boilk'.

'Are you coming to see me? We haven't cuddled all week.'

'Trust me, you don't want to cuddle this.'

And anyway, I couldn't. I'd massively overslept in the hotel and had to be woken by a slightly startled cleaning lady who found me in bed with a Gladiator.

'He's the best man,' I offered by way of alleviation. If anything, that made it worse.

The plan had been to stop off in Manchester for a cuddle before heading back down to Southampton, but I would now have to drive straight to Hampshire, still dressed as Prime. A Search and Rescue team had been sent off to find my liver, but we'd lost radio contact.

'I'll see you tomorrow, though, my lovely. Can I go now please – I'm already multi-tasking by driving and feeling massively sick.'

'I thought you said you weren't going to get drunk?'

'You have to be alive to be drunk. Please, let me go, I think I need to pull over...'

'There's one more thing, honey. We've had a card through the door saying they tried to drop off a BBQ. Do you know anything about this?'

'...Surprise! I got us the same one as Dot as a wedding present. I'll pick it up when I ge...'

'...With what money?' I could feel Betty's face tautening.

'Well, I had to cut a few corners with the wedding car, but I've got Harry to bring his camper van.'

'A camper van? For a wedding car? And a barbecue for a wedding gift?! Are you serious?'

I needed to say something clever.

'...nice meat?'

'I'm a vegetarian, Andrew! Do you even know me at all?!'

'...sorry, Jess, I do kn...'

'Who?! Jess?!'

'No, not Jess - Betty. I know you're not Jess, but I saw Jess this week and I just got confu...'

'You saw Jess this week?! Why did you see Jess this week?

Honey, is there something you want to tell me?'

'No, of course n...I just saw her at a gig briefly. Look, I'm hung-over, my lovely...'

'You saw Jess and you didn't tell me? I can't believe...'

The line went dead.

I pulled over to be sick. It may or may not have been alcohol-related.

**

I got out of the car in Southampton and vomited (Yet another thing ticked off on my list a 'A gazillion things to do before I die').

I sat heavily on the car park tarmac, breathing in sea air and leaking bile through my nostrils. A group of people approached me looking concerned.

'Do you have somewhere to go?'

They blatantly would have thought I was homeless, had I not still been dressed as Optimus Prime.

'Yes, I'm all right. Thank you.'

They gave me some water and a mint to take away the taste, and went on their way. They resurfaced an hour later, gobsmackedly shouting, 'Oh no, it's him!' when I took the stage to headline the show. The word to describe it was 'harrowing'.

I pulled into Cherwell Valley services on the M40, wondering whether I could commit a petty crime, hand myself in to the police and avoid having to drive back home. The smell of petrol as I filled up the tank proved that my liver was still functioning - and still angry with me.

I moped into the kiosk, looking at nothing but my own sense of pity.

'Pump 7?'

'U-huh.'

'£20.00. Start of the new millennium. Easy.'

Wait...

I looked up. He was smiling.

'Nolin! It's you!'

'Sorry? Who's Nolin?'

Of course - his name wasn't really Nolin. Nolin was just the name I'd given him because he looked like he might be named Norman or Colin. His real name, he told me, was Carl. I preferred Nolin.

'I recognised you as soon as you got out of the car. You're one of the few people who ever gave me any credit for my historical knowledge.'

I told him how I'd spent the weeks since our first meeting trying to cajole other tillmasters into playing our game. Nolin looked genuinely moved.

'You don't look very well,' Nolin said, concerned.

'I'm not.'

'Can I treat you to a cure?'

'Eh?'

Nolin smirked, went into the office...and a minute later returned with a mug of hot liquid.

'This should help a bit. Don't let anyone know I gave it to you.'

'Historical buff and apothecarist? You're an impressive man.'

'It's my job,' Nolin stated, incorrectly.

I drank down the fizzy linctus in one. Nolin smiled approvingly.

'Thank you, my friend. May I...may I embrace you, Carl?'

Lifting the hatch of the kiosk counter, Nolin crossed the threshold, and I wrapped my arms round him in gratitude twinned with exhaustion. He still stank like Mo Farah's trainers, but I didn't care. I needed a cuddle.

'Until we meet again,' Nolin said, firmly gripping my hand and slipping me some complimentary breath mints.

I slothed my way out to the car and unlocked Florence the ailing Fiesta. But then a thought struck me. I popped my head back inside the doorway.

'Carl?'

'Yes?'

'...Would you like to come to my wedding?'

I got back to Manchester that night desperate for a full night's sleep and a booster of fizzy tranquillisers. Florence the juddering Fiesta had conked out again en route, and it was the sort of hour when only witches and *BBC2* sign language interpreters were up and about. Pob's light wasn't on, though - he was out, witching in Macaton probably.

The opening of the front door crumpled up the letter that had fallen on to the welcome mat.

I saw the handwriting on the envelope and knew straightaway what it was.

To my Andy,

I'm so sorry, but I can't do it. I can't marry you at the moment.

I love you so much, and I've tried to be patient during the last ten weeks, but it's just caught up with me. I know you'll say the Challenge is practically done, but your lifestyle will always be erratic, honey. You'll always be striving for the next thing. It's not a bad quality, but it won't work for our marriage.

We've come all this way, and I was enjoying it, but all you seem to care about is yourself. This relationship won't work if it's just you in the centre of it.

This barbecue thing...you've spent loads of our money on something I don't want or need, without talking to me.

As for Jess, well, I don't even begin to understand what's happening there, but it all adds up to the point where I think we should just get out while we can. I can't marry a man who refuses to communicate.

I wanted to spend my life with you. But it wouldn't be my life — it would be yours I'd have to work around. It's not fair, Andy. None of this seems fair.

I want the best for you, my love. I'm so sorry to do this to you.

Your Betty
xx

I went and vomited. This time it had nothing to do with alcohol.

Bollocks.

Bollocks bollocks bollocks.

...Bollocks.

**

The retirement flat was clean and quaint, but it was too sterile to feel like home.

He stirred from his nap as I gripped his arm.

'Grandad? It's me. I've brought someone to see you. This is Betty - my girlfriend.'

'Lovely to meet you,' Betty said, beaming down at the man in the chair.

He smiled at Betty and offered her a limp hand.

'My pleasure,' he wheezed.

'Shall I make us all of cup of tea?' Betty asked.

'Good idea,' I effused.

Betty went round the corner into the kitchenette, closed the door and flicked on the kettle.

I sat down next to Grandad and took his hand.

'Before you say anything about her, Grandad, I just want you to know...'

I lowered my voice to a whisper...

'...I'm definitely planning to marry this one.'

But he had already gone back to sleep.

T-Minus 1 Week

"Of all sad words of tongue or pen, the saddest are these, it might have been."
P.G. Wodehouse

Carlos responded to my weekly email with a simple 'See you at the wedding'.
I would probably have to reply.
Later...

Another email had been waiting in my Inbox since the stag do. It offered me a gig in Essex - the only untapped county left on the Backstreet Boys wall chart.
I'd done it. I'd won.
I felt nothing.

I'd woken from fitful sleep hoping the morning might bring clarity or, better still, news of a heartless prank from my former future wife. It did neither.
Surely she would call and say she didn't mean it - that she spoke too hastily? Surely this was salvageable? Surely this couldn't be it?
But there was no contact. I'd spent nearly three months waiting on phone calls and emails from random people I'd never met. I had never been as desperate for a phone call as I was now. The hangover from the stag do had gone, but I felt sick.

'What am I going to do, Tony?' I asked Vino, the one person who always phoned.
'Mate, go and find her. Say sorry, say you'll give it up.'
'The challenge is done, Vino - giving it up won't make any difference.'

'I'm not talking about the challenge, Kindy. I'm talking about comedy.'

I went round to Betty's house. No answer. Maybe she was hiding in the shower? I called and recalled. No answer. She hadn't even changed her voicemail to a more surly version.
This wasn't a joke.
I couldn't find her anywhere, and none of her friends was able to enlighten me. Nobody had seen her.
I lay on the orange velour settee, crying and swearing. Just after midday, Pob slid curiously out of his hole to ask if everything was OK. I told him I'd just lost on *Fifa* and he laughed and slid away.

After a day of fruitless wildgoosing, under duress from my own soul, I gave up the chase.
I went to my gig. My life was in tatters, but I least I knew where to find a comedy club. And after all, it was just what I did. I was a comedian.

XS Malarkey, now in its second decade as a comedy club, remains the centre of the comedy cosmos in the north of England - the gig around which all other gigs orbit. It was the gig that everyone knew about, looked forward to - the gig which comics everywhere held up as an example of what comedy could be. You always judge yourself against your best gig, and some of my best gigs had come at XS. Whenever I wrote material, I always imagined delivering it in front of the assembled mass of connoisseurs at the former Fallowfield train station on Wilmslow Road, Manchester.
I needed XS tonight.

The venue was full and fulsome and pregnant and other lovely words like that. I stood hunched in the Green Room at the back and tried to chat to old friends, Ros and Spider, as though I hadn't just obliterated my future. The fact that I welled up while Spider was talking about his all-time Man City XI suggests I didn't pull it off.

'Georgi Kinkladze was a great player!' I puffed out as a smokescreen.

My old friend Toby Hadoke compered the show. Toby might be the biggest *Dr Who* fan in the universe (or, in fact, any universe, including those written by Moffat or T. Davies). While not physically imposing, and a bit ramshackle in his appearance, his warmheartedness makes him a joy to be around. Like the Tardis, he's bigger on the inside.

'I'll just bring you straight on, Andy - you know what to do.'

I did. If any gig was going to reverse the polarity of my mood, it was going to be XS. Everything was there for comedy. No drunken Vikings, no poultry announcements, no dogs to bite me.

And then, oddly, no laughs.

I did badly. It was the same material that had worked so well on so many occasions in so many counties, but they just didn't laugh. They smiled and watched, and some nodded agreement at the points I was making, but they didn't laugh. The audience did a very good impression of The Silence.

I'd gone to the one gig where I always felt safe, always felt good, always felt like a proper comedian. And I'd died. My favourite stage had become a gallows. Old Lady Stand-Up had brought me to my knees, and I doubted my chances of regenerating.

Lenny Bruce said that 'Comedy is the only honest art form - you can't fake it'. I second that.

Two gigs to...bollocks.

**

Betty had gone to Cambridgeshire to stay with her parents. She wouldn't talk to me, but at least I knew she was safe. I still couldn't find the strength or courage to tell anyone that the wedding was cancelled. *This can't be it.*

I ripped the campaign planner off the wall and bit it. I eviscerated it with tooth and claw and left it ragged on the floor. 'Lost at *Fifa* again, Andy?' Pob asked with an asinine grin. I picked up some shreds of poster and spat them at him. They caught on the air current and landed behind me. #bollocks

Tuesday's gig in Cornwall was that piece of the jigsaw you find behind the radiator when the box has been returned to the loft. That would be a far better analogy if the jigsaw had somehow conspired to ruin your entire life, or if it was *Jumanji*.
I didn't want to play the game anymore. I never wanted to set foot on a stage again.

I had realised what was missing from the performance at XS - why, despite everything being set up for me to rip it, I'd crashed and burned and died: it was joy.
Before Betty came along, comedy had been my pleasure, my first love. But comedy, like football before it, had filled a void that was meant for something else: for relationship. Joy can never be in things - only in people. Now that Betty had gone, and with her joy, I saw Old Lady Stand-Up for what she was: a cheap substitute. A floozy, second-hand hooker at the wrong end of a wedding aisle.

'I'll drive you to Cornwall,' Victor Smithers said.
'No, mate.'
'Yes, mate. I'll drive you and we'll have a road trip. What's better - stay in the flat on your own and beat yourself up, or get away

with a mate?'

'What about your frozen hand?'

'...it's better now.'

So for the first time in his life, Victor Smithers picked me up and drove...all the way to Land's End.

'It's a long drive, Kindy, but don't worry - I've brought with me a meaningful packed lunch.' He gestured to a wicker basket on the back seat. Inside were pork pies, Scotch eggs, Parma ham, sandwiches. I barked with laughter in spite of myself.

'That's not a packed lunch, Victor. That's a picnic.'

It took us nearly seven hours to get to Cornwall. The voice of Debbie, my sat nav, had been the single most consistent voice in my life recently, and her implacable drone had grated away my goodwill. Not once had she told me to turn round and go back, and she should have done. This was her fault, really.

'Are you still determined to give up comedy, Vic?' I asked morosely.

'Well, I've thought about it, Kindy, and no, I'm not.'

'Really?'

'Really. I was working on an exit plan, but then I read something Ronnie Barker said...about a job where the only accreditation you need is to make people laugh being the best job in the world...it just made me realise how lucky we are to do this. So no, I'm going to stick at it for another year - maybe try to get an agent. Those Japanese death robots will still be there in twelve months - although I've checked and I don't actually think they exist yet.'

Step 38 of 39 was a little wine bar perched on the south-westerly tip of the country. From the Green Room, you could see the English Channel lapping its way to the end of the world in tiny, tiny increments. I sat there with a Coke medley, gazing out at nothing.

I was rostered to open the show, with Victor compering and

Tom Wrigglesworth closing.

'Kindy, would it be easier for you to compere and me open?' Victor asked. 'It would mean you could just chat to them a bit, roll out a bit of badinage, and then bring us on - might make it less of a chore.'

'Yeah, man, that would be good – thanks, Victor.'

Victor was ebullient. It's amazing what a bit of hope can do to a man.

Through sheer force of habit, I set my stopwatch for 20.00 minutes. The intro music blared out from the speakers, Victor beatboxed terribly into the off-stage mic and then said, "Ladies and Gentleman of Kernow - would you p-lease welcome to the stage...a man who recently recovered from gout...so if you like gout, you'll love him: Andy Kind!"

I climbed the Steps one more time.

I had no inclination for anything beyond gentle patter with the crowd. I copy-and-pasted some jokes from my hard drive, but I was at the back-end of my comedy shelf-life and my processor was bust. Without my future wifi, I was obsolete.

The stopwatch showed 16.23 when the screen changed and a picture of a googlemapped moon flashed up: "Jen calling". I picked up the phone from the stage and diverted the call.

'Sorry about that,' I told the audience. Victor was stage-left, stretching his hamstrings like an athlete.

Within seconds, the phone vibrated again: "Jen calling".

'Answer it! We'll have a chat,' a bloke at the front table propounded.

I retrieved the phone again, held it up to the mic for the crowd to hear, and pressed "Answer".

'Andrew...?' My sister's voice was soft and reedy...

'...it's Grandad...you need to get to the hospital...he's dying.'

Eighty people at the end of the world fell completely silent.

'...I'm coming,' I said, loosing the microphone, which clanged tinnily to the stage and rolled away.

'Are you nearby?' Jen asked, her words anaemic.

'No...I'm in...oh please, no.'

I was in Cornwall! What the hell was I doing in Cornwall?! What kind of stupid dick, when he needs to be at a hospital in Stoke, is in Cornwall?! To quote every hack comedian of all time: what is that about?!

I found out much later that Tom Wrigglesworth had rallied and, instead of just headlining the show, performed his upcoming Edinburgh show in full, plus an encore. Victor and I weren't there to enjoy it. An hour after finishing a seven-hour drive, we strapped ourselves back in and started another one.

I'd driven to Cornwall thinking things couldn't get any worse. Thinking was for idiots.

'Please, please, please, please, please...'

Victor abused the journey home as though it were a drunken heckler with limited linguistic range. Florence the Fiesta would have expired at the side of the M5 under such strain, but Victor's car tore into the road with unflinching contempt. Every so often, Victor would get overwhelmed with adrenaline and shout things like 'F*** off, roads!'

We reached Stoke in just over four hours, Victor driving me straight into the complex of North Staffs General Hospital.

'I love you, Victor.'

'Me, too. Have a good'un, Kindy.'

I panted my way to the ward and found Mum, Dad and Jen surrounding a doctor.

I'm too late...

Grandad had suffered a heart attack, which had left him

clinging to life. He was still alive, but the doctors were hedging their bets. They would know more in the morning.

I embraced my family and felt the gentle spasms of grief that accost you at times like this.

'Well done for getting back, bro,' Jen whispered.

'I shouldn't have been there in the first place.'

I looked at Grandad through the glass, my breath steaming up the window, beseeching him not to die.

There wasn't enough space in the room where Mum and Dad sat with him, so I huddled foetally on a chair in a hospital corridor, trying not to doze off. Urgent and pensive-looking staff strode past every now and then, some half-smiling at me, some ignoring.

It was like a gig.

The morning came. I must have slept, but my dreams had been of sitting hunched in a hospital corridor. I preferred dreams about wizards.

The doctors came and examined Grandad, then gathered us together to tell us the news.

**

I was sitting on a bench outside the hospital. I was so flipping hungry, and had decided to find the nearest *Wetherspoons* and try to eat twenty sausages. When they asked me what I wanted with the sausages, I would look appalled and say, 'Nothing. Just sausages.' In my state of grief, this was both the best and most funny thing anyone had ever done.

Betty sat down beside me. I didn't realise it was her at first because I was too busy laughing hysterically about the sausage plan.

'Hi,' she said cautiously.

I looked at her and stopped laughing.

'Hi.'

'Jen said you were here.'

'I was about to go and eat twenty sausages.'

'I guessed.'

'Also, I think you've just sat in bird muck.'

'I'll worry about it later.' She stroked me on the bit of the arm where I'd had my tetanus shot in the early nineties.

I unpacked what had happened. How I'd been in Cornwall and got the call on stage. How Victor had decimated the route and sworn at the road. How Grandad would pull through, but would need much closer attention and care from now on.

How she was my joy.

'…I'm sorry I put comedy before you. And I'm sorry I don't communicate very well. And I'm sorry that you've got bird poo on your bottom, and will you marry me? Please - will you just marry me?'

In none of the reveries in which I'd imagined this going down had I ever conceived of prefacing 'Will you marry me' with 'You've got bird poo on your bottom'. I had singularly failed to map out my mind upon my tongue.

What I had forgotten, of course, was that I was loved. In spite of my ear-splicing stupidity, I was loved.

And she said yes.

Then we went to the pub, and I had a burger.

**

D-Day.

At 6:55am, the sunlight groped its way into the Bed and Breakfast and the light and warmth eased my eyes open. My mind needed no help snapping out of fantasy this morning, nor was there any need to give the alarm clock the Vs and go back to sleep for three hours. This was my day - I knew exactly who I was and, for the first time in months, I felt in complete control. I was subservient to no-thing and no-body.

'Morning, Kindy!' Tony was already up, sitting on the edge of his bed, preparing his Best Man speech.

'I'm having some trouble with the speech. I'm thinking of starting like this: "How do you take a very small penis and make it ten times bigger?"'

'Sounds perfect,' I blearily bleared.

The wedding didn't kick off until 3:00pm, so I took life easy. I rose from my bed, chatted (with Tony), had a shower (without Tony), then had a coffee (with Tony). At around 8:00am, the other chosen men dripped down from the upper floors and we all sat on the veranda (Me, Vino, Harry, G-reg) drinking coffee and trumping violently with nerves.

'Shame you didn't get that agent, though, Andy,' Harry sympathised.

'We wouldn't be here if I had, mate.'

'Still,' Vino interjected, 'better to have tried and failed than to have succeeded, got big-headed, and ultimately descended into alcoholism.'

'Cheers to that!' I raised my coffee.

The landlady bustled on to the veranda and brought us all an abattoir's worth of cooked meat.

'For the groom it's free - all the rest of you have to pay.'

A free breakfast - finally! I piled six sausages on to my plate and thought of Richard the weepy waiter. I hoped he hadn't been sacked.

At around 11:00am, with no meat left to digest and nothing else to do, we decided to get changed.

My wedding suit had arrived without trousers, and so I was

wearing my Dad's. My Dad is not the sort of man who likes to lend other men his trousers. He's kind of made that his motto in life and will often bring it up if he feels a conversation has started to lag. Still, I was the groom. This was one day when I would get to have my cake and eat it. And should I get any of that cake on my Dad's trousers, I would wear Tony's (I wish to make it clear that Dad went out and bought a similar shade of trousers for his suit. I wouldn't want you to think that he stood through the service in gaping boxers).

We pitched up to the church early and found punters (I mean guests) already milling about. Martin was there - in his own suit, but still looking a bit like an accountant. Nolin had turned up and was garmented in his choicest finery. He was dressed like a man engaged in trafficking, but he had other qualities outside dress sense. He was chatting to G-reg who had come alone, having not replaced the horrendous girlfriend who nobody liked apart from G-reg.

'I'd love to come and meet you at your office and talk about how we could go about you representing me.' Victor had cornered Carlos as soon as the agent arrived.
'Call my assistant, Diane - she'll book a time,' Carlos responded, unhooking himself from Smithers. Smithers skipped off fist-pumping.
'Good of you to come,' I said to Carlos, offering my hand.
'I'm a man of my word, Andy. All the best for it.'
'Thank you...'

A small mini-bus-cum-van-cum-ambulance pulled on to the church drive, 'Good Hope Retirement Home' printed on the side. A ramp descended and a burly man in green overalls wheeled Grandad on to the gravel. I jogged away from my conversation and went to greet my hero.
'You look very smart today, Grandad,' I declared, kneeling

down beside him. Grandad was indeed looking very smart in his best/only suit. It was cavernously baggy now, but his campaign medals glistened proudly in the sunlight.

'Thank you, son - not as smart as you, though.'

'How are you feeling?' I was speaking loudly (and foolishly so - his heart-attack hadn't affected his hearing).

'Oh fine, fine – looking forward to it.'

'And I finally get to wear this...' I unbuttoned the inside pocket of my blazer and pulled out my ring. His ring.

'...Looks familiar,' Grandad smiled.

'I'm so glad you could be here,' I told him. I allowed a short silence in which neither of us said anything about Gran not being there, but we both thought it.

'Enjoy the service, Grandad. I'll see you later.' I kissed his forehead, dusted off my trousers and started walking away.

'This girl of yours...'

I stopped in my tracks and braced myself.

'Yes...?'

Grandad raised his eyes to meet mine...and smiled.

'She's a good'un. She'll drive you up the wall...but she's a good'un.'

My laughter and tears burst out simultaneously.

The vicar met me at the church doors.

'Afternoon, Andy. Can I run you through some last-minute check-ups?'

Arthur had been the vicar of my childhood church in Stoke. He had long since decamped to Llandudno, but I had wanted to bring him out of retirement for one last hurrah.

It had been a long time. I had envisaged turning up at Arthur's house and his wife Joan would answer and say, 'He's not here - you'll find him in the hills'. I would trek up some narrow, treacherous path, find Arthur sitting cross-legged on the edge of a ravine, and we'd have the following conversation:

'How did you find me, Andy?'

'I have my ways...Joan sent me your address and we satnavved it.'

'Of course, Joan!'

'Listen, Arthur: we need you – we need you for one last service.'

'I'm too old for this sh*t!'

'Damn it, man, you're the best and you know you are!'

'There's no such thing!!'

After this, we'd have some kind of sexy Tae Kwon Do battle, Arthur would floor me and, as he walked away, he'd turn and say in a gravelly voice:

'I'll do it. But after this time, that's it. No more.'

In reality, when I turned up in Wales and asked him to take the service, he replied that he'd be delighted and honoured. If I'm honest, he didn't look cut out for a sexy Tae Kwan Do battle.

The guests started to flock into the church from about 2:30pm. I sat at the front, sipping from the hip-flask that Dad kept passing me under the pew.

'How you feeling?' Vino asked.

'...Ready.' And I was. Louis CK said that being popular with an audience is a rickety ladder to climb. My ladder had had 39 rungs, some firm enough, but quickly followed by rotting, maggot-infested stakes that left me clinging by my fingernails. But I'd been saved - rescued from falling by the knowledge that the only audience that mattered was the small but perfectly formed one en route to me now: the one in the white dress.

'14.58! Matthias Corvinus becomes King of Hungary.'

'Thanks, Nolin.'

'Carl.'

It was indeed two minutes to three. She was nearly here. I was moments away from the biggest biggig of my life.

At 15:03pm, a pimped up VW camper van turned on to the church drive. It was driven by an amoral comedian in a chauffeur's uniform. Arthur the vicar swooshed down the aisle

and gripped my shoulder.
'She's here, Andy.'
I took a final swig of Dad's hip-flask.
'Have a good'un,' mouthed Tony.
'I have, mate. I really have.'

'Would the congregation please stand...'

Grandad spent most of the service asleep in his wheelchair, occasionally rousing briefly when the worship band got particularly loud. My sister Jen sat by him throughout, stroking his arm and giving a commentary of the key moments:
'She's coming down the aisle now.'
'Tony has just fainted.'
'She looks so beautiful.'
'The chauffeur is crying.'
'They're going to do the vows now.'
'There's your ring.'
'Andrew is crying now.'
'Tony's down again.'

**

The new Mr and Mrs Kind were welcomed into the Saffron Walden reception venue with a standing ovation. After the wedding, Harry (acting antithetically to his stag do persona) shepherded guests out of the church and towards the waiting mini-buses.

The catering budget had never been fully tamed and so, as a last resort, the Char-o-matic 2000 Barbecue had been ferried down to Cambridgeshire on the top of a lorry, with a 'Wide Load' sign and a police escort. Burgers were flipped and condiments abused.
'Do you think we should start Burger Saturday?' Tony asked

through beefy jowls.

'I think we already have enough days on our food calendar, mate...why don't we do it on a Tuesday?'

'Tuesday?! Kindy, what the hell is wrong with you?! Tuesday is Kebab Tuesday - always has been, always frickin' will be! That's where the name comes from! I can't believe you're doing this to me - you've finally lo...'

I left Vino reeling and went to get a drink. I passed G-reg on the way, chatting drunkenly to a girl named Suzanne - a lovely girl who everybody liked including G-reg. He was telling her about his work with endangered animals, trying to smile charmingly but, in the way that all smiles do when you're hammered, it came out as a grotesque, lecherous gurn.

Betty PresentKind was mingling with the guests - compering.

'Hello Wifey,' I grinned, hoving in for a cuddle. She didn't Brianodriscoll me, and I wrapped my arms around her and kissed her lovely face.

'I think we're running out of burgers at the BBQ - all your mates are manversusfooding them.'

'Look, Betts, it'll be fine. And anyway, it's time for the speeches.'

My wedding speech lasted twenty minutes. How could it not have done? I ripped it, but then I had pretty much hand-picked the audience. Grandad slept throughout.

Carlos found me at the bar afterwards and beckoned me to one side.

'Here you go,' he said, handing me a cheque for £25.

'Thanks for the wedding gift,' I responded, folding it in two.

'It's not a wedding gift. It's a fee – for the gig you've just done.' His expression was candid.

'Is this a joke?' I asked, baffled. 'Look, Carlos, it's my wedding day - don't rub it in. I failed and it's in the past.'

'Actually, you didn't fail.' I checked his eyes for sarcasm, but there was none.

'I don't get where you're going with this, I'm afraid. I did fail. The wedding speech doesn't count - I've already done Cambridgeshire.'

'Yes, you have. And you got married in Cambridgeshire. But this isn't Cambridgeshire. This is Essex.'

Carlos' signature grin dissected his face with mirth. 'Congratulations.'

'...But no, look...I didn't finish the Cornwall gig and...'

'...Wait. Just wait. I know what happened in Cornwall, and I know you opted out and I know that for you, this isn't a gig. What I also know is that you did everything I asked of you – and a good deal more than I expected!' Carlos downed his pint with ease and slammed the plastic glass down on the bar.

'Andy, I would be delighted to offer you representation on behalf of the Big Fat Comedy Agency. By the time you get back from your honeymoon, there will be a contract waiting for you.'

My mind went back to that day in London ten weeks ago. How much I'd wanted an agent. How angered I had been with Carlos' smug diffidence. How determined I had been to wipe the arrogance off his face.

I'd done it.

Carlos was an influential man within the industry. I would now be able to fulfil my dreams within comedy. Bigger gigs, bigger pay cheques, bigger platforms - I would never have to perform at a bus-stop, supermarket or homeless shelter again.

I looked over to Betty, a picture of joy on her wedding day. Having an agent would mean I could provide for her like never before. We could start our married life with a much-needed financial boost.

'Thanks, Carlos. That's very nice of you,' I said excitedly.

'Excellent. I shall get on with the business of...'

'...But it's a no from me.'

Carlos raised an eyebrow.

'Really, I appreciate the offer, and the integrity behind it. You're a man beyond your words, Carlos.'

I finished my own pint, slammed it down next to his and pointed to my wife (my flipping, joyous, actual wife).

'...But I'd rather have her.'

Carlos met my gaze and nodded. He held out his hand and we shook. Not as partners, nor as friends, but as two men between whom respect had somehow wedged its way.

'But if you're ever in Manchester,' I called after him as he strolled to the car park, '...feel free to pop in for a Tassimo.' He raised a hand, but didn't look back.

The reception wound down and numbers started to dwindle. The wedding speeches had been followed swiftly by a pre-arranged dance-battle. The willing guests formed a circle of dance within the hall, and *Miami* by Will Smith sounded from the iPod. I hip-hopped into the centre and pulled out all my best moves.

I lost.

'We should think about going too, my love,' Betty told me. It was nearly midnight, and only Martin and Nolin were still grooving away.

'Yep. Show's over.'

I brought Florence the 'wearing a new hat' Fiesta round to the front of the venue. She'd had a polish and a spray tan, but she would need scrapping and upgrading once we got back from the New Forest.

'One last trip, Florence. Then you get to rest.'

Jen wheeled Grandad over and I kissed his dozing forehead.

'Sleep well, Grandad.'

The crowd cheered us and threw confetti, and I suitably bowed and unsuitably curtsied. Then, mounted upon my untrusty steed, Florence reared off towards the horizon.

I typed in the address for our honeymoon cottage.

'At the end of the road, go straight on,' Debbie the sat nav instructed - in the voice of Alf from *Home and Away*.

My audience of one held my hand as I left centre-stage and the curtain came down.

I had no idea what the future held. And there would be some difficult career-choices to make soon enough. But they would have to wait. They would just have to wait.

'It'll be fine,' I said out loud.

'What will?' asked Betty.

'It. All of it.'

And it would be.

For the old life had gone; a new life had begun.

With Betty: the great love of my life.

"Applaud my friends, the comedy is over."
Ludwig van Beethoven (his final words)

THE END

A spot of housekeeping...

The Gig Delusion is a novel, not an autobiography. Lots of it is true, but it is not intended as a literal account of that period in the history of the world.

There are various way of numbering English Counties. I have simply taken the 'historical counties' to make it easier for myself.

Huge thanks must go to the following people:

To Peter Cash, for teaching me A-level English, and for proofreading the manuscript, stamping out errors with impunity.

To Dee Williamson, for being my editor and sounding board throughout the process. For encouraging me when bits were good and telling me off when they weren't. To find out more about Dee's work - including editing services - go to www.originaldee.com.

To Mark McKnight at Wilmot Books, for publishing TGD. www.wilmotbooks.co.uk

To all the staff at The Anchor Coffee House (Whitworth Park, Manchester), for plying me with endless cups of caffeine and Lemon Drizzle cake.

To Hannah Prittie, for the wonderful work she did with the cover. www.hannahbeatrice.co.uk

To Alex Willmott, for taking on the role of Press Officer.

To all the comics I've mentioned in here. May you forever have a good'un.

To Victor Smithers, for not existing.

Finally, To Eric Wilmot Kind and John Louis Rowley. I wish I'd known you longer.

To contact Andy:

andy@andykind.co.uk

@andykindcomedy on Twitter

Lightning Source UK Ltd.
Milton Keynes UK
UKOW050401270513

211265UK00001B/1/P